THE TEACHING OF MATHEMATICS

THE TEACHING OF MATHEMATICS

A. E. ASHWORTH B.Sc., M.Ed.
READER IN CURRICULUM AND
TEACHING STUDIES,
CHANCELLOR COLLEGE, UNIVERSITY OF MALAWI

HODDER AND STOUGHTON
LONDON SYDNEY AUCKLAND TORONTO

British Library Cataloguing in Publication Data

Ashworth, A E
   The teaching of mathematics.
   1. Mathematics – Study and training (Elementary)
   I. Title   II. Series
   372.7'3'044   QA135.5

ISBN 0 340 25953 1

First Published 1981
Fourth impression 1986
Copyright © 1981 by A. E. Ashworth

All rights reserved. No part of this publication may be
reproduced or transmitted in any form or by any means,
electronic or mechanical, including photocopy, recording, or
any information storage or retrieval system, without
permission in writing from the publisher.

Represented in West Africa by
Nigeria Publishers Services Ltd, P.O. Box 62,
Ibadan, Nigeria.

Phototypeset in V.I.P. Plantin by
Western Printing Services Ltd, Bristol

Printed and bound in Great Britain
for Hodder and Stoughton Educational,
a division of Hodder and Stoughton Ltd,
Mill Road, Dunton Green, Sevenoaks, Kent
by Biddles Ltd, Guildford and King's Lynn

CONTENTS

Preface viii

Chapter One
The Teacher's Task 1
Lesson Plan – Title of the Lesson – Aim of the Lesson – Knowledge Assumed – Teaching Aids – Introduction to the Lesson – Procedure – Children's Tasks – Organizational Considerations – Evaluation – Self Criticism – Summary – Exercises, Assignments and Projects.

Chapter Two
Organizing the Year's Teaching 14
The Teacher's Syllabus – Time Available – Lesson Titles – Exercises, Assignments and Projects.

Chapter Three
Why Do We Teach Mathematics? 22
Mathematics for Life – Mathematics and Other Subjects – Other Aims in Teaching Mathematics – Social Training – Exercises, Assignments and Projects.

Chapter Four
Teaching and Learning Aids 30
Teaching Numbers 1 to 9 – Place Value – Fractions – Area of a Triangle – Exercises, Assignments and Projects.

Chapter Five
Different Methods of Teaching Mathematics 44
The Didactic or Formal Approach – Formal Demonstration – Teacher Demonstration, Class Conclusion – Conducted Class Discussion – Conducted Discovery – Discovery Approach – Discussion of Methods of Teaching – Variety – Exercises, Assignments and Projects.

Chapter Six
Examples of Lessons Prepared in Some Detail for Different Ages 55
Primary 1: Fractions – Primary 2: Addition of Two Digit Numbers – Primary 3: Multiplication – Primary 4: L.C.M. – Primary 5: Money – Primary 6: Volume – Exercises, Assignments and Projects.

Chapter Seven
Organizing Children's Work 70
Classwork – Homework – Exercise Books – Note Books – Procedure – Vocabulary – Notes – Notes for Revision – Exercises, Assignments and Projects.

Chapter Eight
Evaluation 83
Can we make tests to find out what the children are having difficulty with? – Can we make tests to group children into sets? – How do we know if a question is difficult or not? – Does the difficulty level tell us anything else? – Can we construct a test to find the children requiring remedial treatment? – Can we construct a test to find the very bright child? – Can we make tests which will give us reliable information on the achievements of children so that our reports to parents are meaningful? – Can we check that our tests are reliable and valid? – Did our test achieve its purpose? – Reporting to

Parents – Can we ensure that our tests help students to learn rather than help to destroy their confidence? – Are tests available which we can use so that we can compare the ability of our with children of similar ages? – Exercises, Assignments and Projects.

Chapter Nine
Records and Classroom Organization 99
Records – Organization in the Classroom – Exercises, Assignments and Projects.

Chapter Ten
Difficulties Met by the Student Teacher and the New Teacher 106
Teaching Practice – Discipline – Organizing Yourself – The New Environment – What and When You Have To Teach – Equipment – The Children – General Rules and Organization – Teaching Methods – The Area around the School – The New Teacher – Exercises, Assignments and Projects.

Chapter Eleven
Evaluating Our Teaching 110
List of Questions To Ask – Exercises, Assignments and Projects.

Chapter Twelve
Revision Questions 115

Sources of Information and Materials 117

Preface

Mathematics can be fun and yet if we enquire about the attitudes of children to mathematics we find that in most schools mathematics is not among the more popular subjects. When we find children who do enjoy mathematics and ask them 'why' the main reason they give is that they 'get it right'. They regard mathematics as a puzzle; when they achieve understanding and solve the puzzle they feel successful and pleased with themselves. The aim of this book is to put forward some ideas which it is hoped will help the mathematics teacher to organize a successful learning situation where the children can achieve understanding and enjoy mathematics.

This is no easy task. A teacher must be prepared to work hard to achieve this aim. Mathematics is an abstract subject: a different language is used to convey ideas. We use shorthand (symbols) to explain new concepts. Often the children are not sufficiently conversant with the language and concepts used and hence do not understand the new concept we are trying to explain. As many topics in mathematics rely on the understanding of previous topics (i.e. it is a logical subject) a gap in the knowledge of a particular child can make it impossible for him to learn future topics. This leads to failure and frustration and often a hatred of the subject. Mathematics must be taught in a logical order and the teachers must ensure that the child's previous knowledge is sufficient for him to understand the next step.

It is impossible to answer all the problems of a mathematics teacher in the space allowed for this book. It is hoped to explain how a teacher can produce good lessons. Some primary topics will be covered in some detail and it is hoped that by studying these topics the teacher will be able to prepare other topics along similar lines.

As the main concern of the teacher is to produce successful lessons the book is written with this problem continually in mind. The first chapter puts forward a general plan for lesson preparation. Subsequent chapters explain in more detail the thoughts a teacher should have as he is preparing his lessons. Where space allows, concrete examples are given to illustrate points made. As all topics in the primary school cannot be covered you should regard this book as a source of thoughts which should start you thinking about how to teach mathematics successfully. As there are many different methods of teaching you have to decide how many and which of the methods explained are relevant to your particular situation and can be successfully used by you. A topic will be taken to show how the same content may be taught by different methods. The problems met by the trainee teacher on teaching practice and teachers in their first teaching post are discussed. Special emphasis is given to the introductory lessons dealing with fundamental concepts of mathematics taught in the primary school.

If you show the children that you enjoy teaching mathematics you will be half way to showing them how to enjoy the subject too. You cannot enjoy teaching mathematics unless you know the content well, are aware of the difficulties in understanding a particular topic and have produced a means of communicating these ideas successfully to young minds.

Chapter One

The Teacher's Task

Many people dismiss the problems of the Primary Mathematics teacher by saying, 'Oh, they don't have to do very much, just teach the children how to add, subtract, multiply and divide. There's nothing very difficult about that!' This, however, is very far from the truth. The first few years of the child's experience with mathematics are crucial. They can affect the child's attitude to mathematics for the rest of his life. If a child does not reach a satisfactory understanding of the basic mathematical concepts taught in the primary school, there is little chance that he will achieve any success in the more advanced areas of this subject. The primary school teacher shoulders the responsibility of producing children who have well formed basic concepts and who are able to use these concepts to further their knowledge of mathematics.

In order to achieve this the teacher must have a good understanding of the concepts to be taught. He must be able to present these concepts to the children in a way which will be easily understood and assimilated by them. He must show the children how to apply these concepts and, subsequently, how to use these concepts to develop further concepts.

Before we look in detail at how particular topics can be taught, we will look at a general plan which should be useful in lesson preparation. Each step in the lesson plan will be discussed in more detail in subsequent chapters.

Lesson Plan

If the teacher enters the classroom with no clear idea of what he is going to do during the lesson the children will soon realise this and give him the attention he deserves! If a teacher has spent time on his preparation he will walk into the classroom with a purpose; he will not want to feel that his preparation time is wasted. He will strive to communicate his ideas with enthusiasm and he will insist on concentration and hard work from the children. The children's own attitude to a subject often reflects the attitude of the teacher.

Until you have had some experience in teaching, the best way to achieve this level of preparation and confidence is to follow a plan which will make you think about the different parts of the lesson.

The lesson plan discussed below should be regarded as something to think around. Depending on the methods of teaching you use you may find that after you have used the plan for some time you wish to adapt it.

The first thing the teacher must decide is what he is going to teach.

Title of the Lesson

This sounds very easy but a great deal of work must be done before a teacher can write down the title of the lesson.

In many schools a teacher will be supplied with a list of topics to be covered during the year. The teacher is left to decide for himself the order in which he is going to teach them and the amount of time he will give to each topic. At the beginning of the school year the teacher should prepare a sketch plan of the whole year's work before he even begins to think about what he is going to teach in his first lesson. He should divide the material into lesson units, give each lesson a title and give some estimate of the number of class periods he will require to cover each lesson.

When a teacher has decided what he is going to teach in a particular lesson he should write down the title and then question himself to see if he has a good concept of the title. You will quite often find that you cannot explain clearly what the title means. You can blame this on your own education but this will not help the children you are teaching.

Let us consider some examples.

Example 1

Consider the title of your lesson is 'area'.

What do you mean by the word 'area'? Write down what you think you mean by the word. Now 'look up' the word in the dictionary. Compare your definition with the dictionary definition. Compare your definition with other definitions written by members of your group. Find out how many students used the word 'space' in their definition of area. Area is surface – volume is the amount of space – we should never use the word space when talking about area.

Example 2
Consider you are going to teach 'fractions'.
Try and write down what you mean by the term 'a simple fraction'. A good definition might be, 'a simple fraction is a numerical quantity that is not a whole number. It is expressed by a numerator above a line and a denominator below that line. The denominator indicates the number of parts into which the whole was divided and the numerator indicates the number of those parts which are now present.'
How does this definition compare with your own?

Example 3
Consider that you are going to teach 'decimals'.
Try to write down what you mean by the term 'a decimal'. Check your definition with the one in your mathematics book. How did your definition compare with the one in the book?

When you try to write down what you mean by a mathematical topic you will often discover that you don't always know the full meaning of the topic yourself. When you write down the title of your lesson you should always write down the meaning of the title as well.

Aim of the Lesson

When a teacher has decided what he is going to teach he should think for a few minutes about why he is teaching the topic at all. If the teacher is not convinced of the usefulness of a particular topic he will plod through the lesson in an aimless way and will not capture the interest of the children. If he can see why the lesson is important, he will conduct his lesson in a more purposeful way. The children will reflect the teacher's attitude. They will try to follow the lesson and will make some effort to remember what they have been taught. Where possible, the children should be shown that what they are being taught is going to be useful, either immediately or later when they study more difficult topics in mathematics. As far as possible the subject matter should be used to develop practical or cognitive skills in the children. A teacher should always try to develop such an interest in his subject that the children will carry on their learning activities outside the classroom. A wise teacher will include topics which he knows the children will enjoy and have fun with.

The teacher's answer to why he is teaching a particular lesson will affect his whole approach to his preparation and presentation. This will be discussed in some detail in subsequent chapters.

Knowledge Assumed

Before the teacher starts the actual preparation of the lesson he should consider what knowledge he can assume the children already have. His lesson will not be followed with interest if he is repeating material the children have already learned. If he assumes too much, however, the children will have too many difficulties to overcome and will soon become bored or lose interest altogether.

Let us consider an example. We wish the children to state some properties of plane shapes, for example of the triangles (equilateral and isosceles), parallelogram, trapezium and rhombus. We assume that:
- (a) the children know the names of the shapes;
- (b) they know the meaning of the terms 'parallel', 'opposite', 'equal' and 'perpendicular';
- (c) they are able to draw the shapes.
    (We may wish the children to cut out the shapes so we may want to assume that the children are able to use scissors with some amount of skill.)

When we analyse the situation we realize that we have assumed quite a lot. If the same teacher has taught all of the above he will have a fairly good idea of what the children know and can do. If the children are new to him it may be necessary to give them a pre-test to find out exactly what they do know.

Teaching Aids

When the teacher has decided what he is going to teach, why he is teaching the topic and where he is going to begin, he can start thinking about how he is going to communicate his ideas.

He should consider which Teaching Aids or Learning Aids he will use to improve his ability to communicate his ideas. The teaching aids most useful to a mathematics teacher are the blackboard, text books, the children's exercise books, duplicated materials, mathematical instruments, two and three dimensional models, counters, cards, graph paper, wall charts, etc. These and other teaching aids will be discussed in more detail in subsequent chapters.

If the class consists of children with a wide ability range the teacher may decide to produce different learning aids for different groups of children. Teaching aids are of particular use when a teacher wishes to repeat a topic taught previously, which has not been completely understood. If the teacher changes the method of teaching and the aids used, the children often will not realize that the material is being repeated, and will enjoy the repeated lesson. The order in which the headings for lesson preparation are placed cannot be regarded as fixed. It is useful to consider aids at this stage but we may wish to add to the list of aids after the procedure for the lesson has been worked out. Similarly we may change some of our aims when we decide on the method of teaching we are going to use.

Introduction to the Lesson

The teacher should now begin to think about the form the lesson should take. It is necessary to look at the introduction of the lesson separately from the procedure as the introduction sets the atmosphere for the whole lesson. Children often decide in the first few minutes of the lesson whether they are going to be interested or not. They sometimes decide they are going to take as little notice as possible and then they become passengers rather than participants. They may even become a disruptive influence in the classroom! During the first few minutes of the lesson the teacher has to convince the children that he thinks the subject matter is important, that he himself is interested in it and that he thinks it is of some interest, relevance and importance to the children. He should show how the lesson is linked with work done in previous lessons. He should give a brief idea of the amount of work to be covered in the lesson and how it is to be dealt with. The children should know the story of the lesson, they should know what they are going to do and where they are going to be 'led'. We all like to know what we are doing and in which direction we are going.

Many teachers use the introductory period of the lesson to find out if the 'knowledge assumed' was correct. Generally speaking this is not a good idea. The teacher should *know* how much knowledge to assume before he embarks on the lesson. If he leaves it to the lesson to find out he may find himself in the position of having to teach the knowledge he had wrongly assumed the children had. He may find himself teaching material for which he is totally unprepared or to which he has never given any thought until that moment.

Procedure

The teacher's next task is to analyse the subject matter to be communicated. He should divide the content into as small sections as possible. He should recognize the points where he thinks the children may have some difficulty in following the lesson. He should consider the order in which the points of the lesson should be covered. He should consider if certain points should be repeated in a different form in the same lesson to ensure that the children do understand them. He should consider the best way to connect the different points of the lesson so that they make a 'story'. He should produce a summary of the lesson so that he knows what he will expect the children to have learned by the end of it and as a reference for the future.

When the teacher has a very clear picture of the subject matter to be learned he should then decide how he will present the material. Different topics lend themselves to different methods of teaching. There are an infinite number of ways in which a lesson can be presented. To give some idea of the spectrum of teaching methods let us now consider six of those methods and see for ourselves the differences in their approach and the amount of children's involvement in each case.

The Didactic or Formal Approach

This is the method used most often in the teaching of mathematics. The teacher prepares his talk and he presents the material to the class in a logical sequence. He will usually make use of the blackboard to help him to do this. Next he questions the children to find out whether they have understood the concepts involved and he will work through several examples (on the blackboard) or problems involving the process which has just been taught. Then he will set the children some work to do on their own. The teacher lectures rather than teaches.

Formal Demonstration

In this method also the teacher is in complete control of the presentation of material to be taught. The teacher puts forward a problem, shows the children one or more ways in which the problem could be tackled; he demonstrates an experiment with models or with mathematical instruments on the blackboard to show how the problem is solved, he summarizes the conclusions, asks questions and then sets work to be done when he is sure the children have understood.

Teacher Demonstration, Class Conclusion

In this method the teacher prepares a problem, demonstrates any experimental work but allows the children to draw their own conclusions and make their own summary. The teacher will have to find out whether each child has drawn the correct conclusion before he gives them problems which require them to use the knowledge they have just gained.

Conducted Class Discussion

The teacher prepares a problem which is then discussed by teacher and class together. They discuss what experiments or manipulations should be undertaken and the teacher demonstrates the experiments. The children discuss the results and draw their own conclusions. The teacher checks the conclusions of each child and then gives out work which requires them to use the knowledge they have just gained.

Conducted Discovery

The teacher proposes a problem, the teacher and the children discuss the problem (or the children are divided into groups to discuss the problem) and experiments are suggested. The children then carry out the experiments. In this situation different groups may suggest different experiments and they should be allowed to try them. The results of all the experiments are then collected on the blackboard. The children draw their own conclusions from the information they have and their conclusions are again checked by the teacher before any work is assigned.

Discovery

In this method each child proposes his own problem. The problem is discussed with the teacher. The child on his own or with a small group of children carries out experimental work and draws his own conclusions. The teacher must keep detailed notes of each child's progress and after each day the teacher must consider how each child might develop his ideas in the next lesson.

As one progresses from the first method to the last you may have noticed that the child's involvement in the lesson increases. In the discovery approach the child is completely involved throughout. This is sometimes called the child centred method.

Later in this book we will discuss some mathematical topics and show how the same topic can be taught using one or more of the above methods. It must be stressed at this point that the author does not advocate the use of the discovery approach during teaching practice or even in the early part of the first year of teaching. The discovery approach can be successful only when the teacher knows each child and he has had time to prepare both problems and the equipment required to solve those problems to cover the whole year's work. The teacher must be confident that he can control the class during experimental work before he attempts to use the discovery approach. If the children he is teaching have never been taught by the discovery method then he must slowly change his method from the formal approach and proceed slowly through the other five methods so that the children become confident in their own ability to analyse problems and suggest solutions. This will be discussed in more detail in Chapter Five.

You may have heard of other methods, such as the team teaching method, and the group teaching method. These names have been given to certain ways in which the class is organized. To make any discussion on methods even more complicated, different names have been given to basically the same method; for example, the first method is often called the lecturing method, the fourth method the questioning method, and the sixth method the play way method. These methods will also be discussed in Chapter Five.

The method chosen will affect the whole presentation of the lesson. The objectives attained will also depend on the method used. A teacher should give serious thought to which method he uses, depending on the content to be taught.

When the teacher has decided which teaching method he is going to use he should make brief notes on how he is going to conduct his lesson. These notes are not really concerned with the subject matter of the lesson. The subject matter should be in the teacher's mind. The notes should show the order of the lesson and should show how difficult points in the lesson are going to be dealt with and how information is going to be communicated to the children.

Children's Tasks

It can be seen from the last section that the children's tasks in a lesson may be different depending on the teaching method used. The teacher may have decided what tasks the children were going to do when he was preparing his lesson. The teacher should now give this aspect of the lesson his special consideration. The whole point of the lesson is that the children learn something and are able to use their newly acquired knowledge as soon as possible. It is essential that he spend some time considering what he expects the children to do at the end of the lesson. If problems are to be set then consideration should be given to the grading of the questions. If the children are going to be asked to write notes on the experiments done by the teacher or by themselves then the teacher must give them some guidance in how to write the notes and show the children what kind of notes he wants them to write.

If tasks are set for homework the teacher must be sure that they are within the children's capabilities. There is nothing more frustrating for a child than to discover he is unable to start his homework. Homework should always be a repetition of the work done in class and is intended to consolidate the children's knowledge. This is not the time to be giving the child new challenges. A useful question for the teacher to ask at this stage is what use he expects the children to make of their exercise books. Should the children have more than one exercise book? If you have had the opportunity to look at the mathematics exercise books in some schools the only conclusion you may have come to is that they should be thrown away! The majority of children use their exercise books to jot down a few numbers in order to do some calculations and produce an answer. When these exercise books are looked at again later they do not make any sense at all.

Suggestions as to how exercise books should be used will be discussed later.

Organizational Considerations

When a teacher has decided what he is going to teach and how he is going to teach the children, he should give some thought to what materials etc. he needs to prepare before the lesson begins. Many hours of valuable teaching time are wasted because teachers try to organize materials during their lessons. Children get bored during this time and and then the teacher has a difficult time trying to regain their attention. The teacher never has the right to waste children's time. Efficiency should be the key word of every teacher. He should give consideration to such problems as how to give out paper quickly, whether the position of desks in the classroom could be changed to enable himself and the children to move about the classroom more easily, whether the collection of books and materials could be done more efficiently, whether the children's help can be enlisted to make the general organization of the class any easier. The children need to look after the equipment in the classroom and their own mathematical sets. How can the teacher ensure that this will be done?

Evaluation

At the end of each lesson the teacher should make some attempt to evaluate what the children have learned. He will want to know where he should start next lesson. It is not wise for a teacher to assume that because he has covered a topic in a lesson that all the children have learned and understood that topic. The evaluation can be carried out in many ways. The teacher may ask oral questions at the end of the lesson. If he uses this method the teacher must be aware of the fact that children are very skilful in pretending that they understand so that the teacher will be pleased with them. The work the children have done during the lesson may be looked over by the teacher in order to establish the rate of their progress. The teacher may wish to give the children some homework with the view to collecting it and marking it before the next lesson. From time to time it is useful for the teacher to give the children tests covering the work done over a certain length of time. In this way he can see whether the children have really understood what they have been taught before proceeding any further. Evaluation will be discussed in more detail in Chapter Nine.

The teacher should keep records of each child's work; notes and comments on the difficulties a child has experienced are of much more use than just a record of marks. The main reason a teacher marks work and gives tests is to find out the difficulties each child has so that he can help him to achieve understanding. When a teacher constructs a test or sets the children work he should bear in mind that he should be testing not merely knowledge. He should select items for the test which will show whether the children are able to use the knowledge they have. He should test to see if the children can analyse and create something new within the knowledge they have. How to construct tests and the use of tests will be discussed in detail in future chapters.

Self Criticism

This can hardly be considered as part of the lesson preparation but it could be considered as the first step for the preparation of the same topic next year or even for the next lesson. One of the real advantages of being a teacher is that usually you are left to your own devices in the classroom to get on with teaching in whatever way you please. This freedom, however, brings with it certain responsibilities. There is no-one to tell the teacher what he is doing wrong. There is no-one to tell him how to improve his teaching. A good teacher develops the habit of criticizing his own teaching each time he comes out of the classroom. He first of all makes a note of the point reached at the end of the lesson. There is nothing which annoys children more than a teacher who goes into a class and asks 'where did we get up to last time?' before he starts the lesson. It is obvious from that remark that the teacher hasn't given the children a moment's thought since the last lesson.

The teacher should also make notes of the difficulties encountered in communicating his ideas. When he is preparing the same lesson the following year he will find these notes

invaluable. Here is a list of questions a teacher may usefully ask himself when he has left a particular class.
- (a) Did the children enjoy the lesson?
- (b) Did the children understand the lesson?
- (c) Was a pleasant atmosphere obtained?
- (d) Was time wasted? Could things have been better organized?
- (e) Did the blackboard look untidy at the end of the lesson or did it show a neat summary of the main points of the lesson?
- (f) Have the children taken notes of one form or another to which they can refer if they find they need to refresh their memories?
- (g) Did you find yourself going over one point several times because the children didn't understand?
- (h) Do you think the children respect you more or less after the last lesson?

Summary

The main headings of the lesson plan are shown below.
Class ......Amount of time ......No. in class ......Date ......
- (a) Title
- (b) Aims
- (c) Knowledge assumed
- (d) Teaching aids
- (e) Introduction
- (f) Procedure
- (g) Children's tasks
- (h) Organizational considerations
- (i) Evaluation
- (j) Self criticism

These headings are to help the teacher to prepare his lesson and should not be thought of as a set of steps to be dealt with in sequence and then dispensed with.

The teacher must select a topic before he can start. He may have some thoughts on aims from the title but he may not be able to write down all his aims until he has decided which method he is going to use to present the subject matter. Again he may have some thoughts about teaching aids but he will not be able to make a complete list until he has worked out his procedure. The plan should be considered as a framework around which a teacher can base his thoughts whilst preparing his lesson.

Exercises, Assignments and Projects

1. Explain what you mean by
   - (a) area
   - (b) volume
   - (c) a standard measurement
   - (d) a parallelogram
   - (e) a kite
   - (f) a graph.

   Obtain a primary school syllabus and see if you can explain what you mean by the headings given to each topic.

2. It has often been said that 'it doesn't matter what subject we teach but how we teach it'. Discuss the meaning of this statement; make it clear to what extent you think the statement is true. Answer this question again after you have read Chapter Three.

3. State what knowledge you would assume if you were going to teach a lesson on
   - (a) squares and parallelograms,
   - (b) the area of a triangle,
   - (c) long multiplication,
   - (d) percentages.

4. Teaching aids are essential in the teaching of mathematics. Discuss to what extent you think this is true.

5. Give a description of the introduction you would give for two of the following topics
   - (a) area
   - (b) parallel lines
   - (c) simple scale drawing
   - (d) angles.

   Remember in the introduction you have to catch the child's interest and convince him the topic is worth studying.

6. Write a list of questions which you think a teacher could usefully ask himself at the end of a lesson with an aim of improving his teaching.

7. Choose any mathematics topic in the primary syllabus. Use the plan given in the summary to prepare a lesson.

Chapter Two

Organizing the Year's Teaching

The Teacher's Syllabus
The amount of work required to organize your year's teaching depends to a large extent on your starting point.

Whilst inspecting schools I have found teachers who have been given the following syllabus for Primary I:

Primary I
- A. Number   can apply and record addition and subtraction to 10.
- B. Money   can pay for one or more articles up to a total of 9 units.
- C. Measure   can measure lengths using a simple rule.
- D. Weighing   can appreciate different objects have different weights.
- E. Time   can tell the time in hours.
- F. Shapes   can appreciate there are different shapes.
- G. Graphs   can produce form of graph by laying objects side by side.

The amount of work a teacher would have to put into organizing his year's work from such a syllabus is so great that the teacher usually ignores the syllabus and blindly follows a standard textbook.

Consider that you have been given the above syllabus and have been asked to teach Primary I. Write a more detailed syllabus for yourselves. To help you here is a start:

A. *Number*
1. Can match similar objects.
2. Can sort a collection of objects in groups.
3. Can appreciate some groups contain more objects than other groups.
4. Can attach number names to small groups of objects.
5. Can use words such as bigger than and smaller than.
6. ......

Carry on for yourselves. You may find it useful to study several Primary I school texts and see the order in which they teach the syllabus.

Make a collection of primary school syllabuses, and see how they break up the topics. Do they all recommend the same order of teaching? If you find they recommend differences in the order of teaching try and decide which order you think is the best.

When we have produced a detailed syllabus we have only begun our task of organizing the year's work. Let us consider one topic in the detailed syllabus we started above: 'Can attach number names to small groups of objects'. We have now to ask ourselves how we are going to teach this topic, what materials will we need, how many lessons will it take to teach this topic, will different children require different experiences to learn this topic? At this stage you may begin to wonder if you want to teach at all!

Luckily in Africa a great deal of work has been done on the organization of the primary school mathematics syllabus.

For example in 1971 a National Primary School Curriculum Workshop was held in Ibadan University, Nigeria. Reports were produced on the teaching of all primary subjects. A detailed suggested syllabus was produced for the teaching of mathematics in the primary school. See if there is a copy in your library. If not try and obtain a copy.

The headings the group concerned with producing the detailed syllabus used to help in their deliberations were as follows:

A. topic to be taught
B. objectives of teaching
C. the skills to be learnt
D. suggested activities
E. new vocabulary to be learnt
F. materials which might be usefully used
G. additional remarks.

Use these headings; see if they help you to produce a detailed syllabus on a topic of your own choice.

Unfortunately this workshop was held when modern mathematics was being taught in primary school. In consequence some of the sections are now irrelevant. Many of the sections however are relevant and the study of the report should help you to see how to organize a topic.

An extract of the report showing Numeration in Primary II is shown on the following page.

The heading 'Vocabulary' is one which is often forgotten. New words and their meanings have to be learnt in all subjects. On numerous occasions in mathematics we expect students to remember a new word, its meaning, and a symbolic representation of the word after we have explained it once or twice. A teacher should be aware of every new word he is introducing and make sure the children know its meaning.

During Easter 1978 a National Workshop, consisting of representatives of all States in Nigeria, various Educational Institutions and professional organizations met in Onitsha, under the chairmanship of Professor Ezeilo, Vice Chancellor of the University of Nigeria, to consider documents presented by the Nigerian Educational Research Council. The outcome of this meeting was the production of a forty-one page document presenting the new primary syllabus for approval.

An extract of one section of the report for Primary III is shown on page 18.

Starting to organize the year's teaching from a detailed syllabus like this is so much easier. Try and obtain a copy of the report. Keep the report safely until you start teaching. You should keep one file in which you place any documents which you collect during your teacher training period which you decide will be useful when you start teaching.

If you study the extracts from the two reports you will notice that in the second report the number of columns has been reduced. Skills and vocabulary have been omitted. See if you can write the skills and vocabulary columns to accompany this report. Do you think the consideration of skills and vocabulary will help you to teach the topic better?

As you can see from the study of these sections of the report they are most helpful. The Committees have done a great deal of the work for us.

Before spending time working on a topic such as producing a teaching syllabus always find out what work has already been done. When you start teaching try and keep up to date with curriculum development work in mathematics.

National Primary School Curriculum Workshop 1971

TOPICS	OBJECTIVE	SKILLS	ACTIVITIES	VOCABULARY	MATERIALS	REMARKS
B. NUMERA-TION	1. To revise number names and numerals 1–1000. 2. To revise the idea of place value to numerals up to 1000. 3. To expand the idea of ordering numbers (1–1000) using the number line. 4. To revise and expand the idea of ordinal numbers. 5. To develop, counting by twos, fives, tens, twenties, fifties and hundreds up to 1000. 6. To introduce the idea of odd and even numbers from counting by twos. 7. To locate and to compare in pairs fractions $\frac{1}{2}, \frac{1}{4}, \frac{1}{8}, \frac{1}{3}, \frac{1}{6}$, on the number line. 8. To understand that the same fraction has many different names. 9. To use local Nigerian numeration up to 100 and read number words up to 10.	Ability to read, write and count up to 1000. Ability to read and use local Nigerian numeration up to 100. Ability to read number words in local Nigerian language up to 10. Ability to recognize equivalent fractions and to compare pairs of fractions on the number line. Children must be able to count starting from any number. Children must be able to skip count by twos, fives, up to 100 and by 100's up to 1000.	Separating sets of sticks into subjects of tens members. Ordering sets by the number of their members. Using numerals for tens and ones. A numberline with 1 to 10 and beyond. Locating numerals on the hundred-pocket chart. Deciding which of two numbers is greater. Using the signs for 'greater than' and 'less than'. Using the ordinals. Locating the position of $\frac{1}{2}, \frac{1}{4}, \frac{1}{8}, \frac{1}{3}, \frac{1}{6}$, on the number line.	Odd, even, thousand, one half, halves, one-fourths, fourths, thirds, sixths, eighths. Number line. Number names. First, second, . . . , one hundredth. Next, last.	Calendar, hundred-pocket chart. Numeral cards. (0, $\frac{1}{8}$ & $\frac{1}{4}$, $\frac{1}{2}$, 1, $\frac{1}{3}, \frac{1}{6}$). Square numeral and sign cards. Counters.	Drill the children.

17

National Primary School Curriculum Workshop Easter 1978

TOPIC	OBJECTIVES	CONTENT	SUGGESTED ACTIVITIES AND MATERIALS	REMARKS
D. PRACTICAL DESCRIPTIVE GEOMETRY	Pupils will be able to: (i) identify and count the flat faces, corners and edges of cube and cuboid	Properties of cube, cuboid, cylinder and spheres – faces, corners, edges.	Examination and physical handling of cubes, cuboids, cylinders and spheres to recognize and count the following: (i) faces (for all) (ii) corners (cube and cuboid only) (iii) edges (cube and cuboid) (iv) curved faces (sphere and cylinder). Models of these shapes in realistic forms – boxes, tins, balls, etc. should be made available. Also cardboard models of cubes (and possibly cylinders) should be made and dismantled to show flat faces. Skeleton models of cubes and cuboid (made, for example, with drinking straw or corn stalk) will help pupils in counting the number of edges correctly. *Materials* – Various models of three-dimensional shapes.	It is advisable that some construction of models be done by the teacher in the presence of pupils Active participation of pupils in these activities is very essential.
	(ii) identify square, rectangle, circle and triangle (iii) tell which corner of a two-dimensional shape is a square corner.	(i) square, rectangle, circle and triangle (ii) square corners in shapes.	By examining the models of cubes, cuboids and cylinders pupils will be guided to discover the square faces, rectangular faces of cubes and cuboids, and circular faces of cylinders. Circular faces can also be shown by slicing spherical objects like orange or rubber ball. By joining three non-collinear points, draw different types of triangles and make pupils know that a triangle has three sides and three corners. Bring cut-out of plane shapes – square, rectangle, and triangle – and get pupils to count the number of sides of square, rectangle and triangle and also discover square corners in them. Let them also discover that there are corners (for example, in triangles) that are not square. Get pupils to show square corners in classroom objects e.g. exercise books, chalk box face, face of	Pupils should discover that a circle has no straight side. Its side is curved round.

In Nigeria the main bodies concerned with curriculum development work in mathematics are
1. The Nigerian Educational Research Council (NERC), P.O. Box 8058, Yaba, Lagos.
2. The Mathematics Teachers' Association of Nigeria (MTAN).
3. The Mathematics Association of Nigeria (MAN).
4. The West African Examination Council (WAEC), The Senior Deputy Registrar, WAEC, PMB 1022, Yaba, Lagos.

Time Available

Even with the help of these detailed syllabuses our task is not finished. We must count the number of school weeks in the year and multiply by the number of periods given to the study of mathematics (usually 5) per week and hence find the total number of hours we have in which to teach the syllabus. This sounds quite simple and yet in practice we have much less teaching time.

Suppose we have three terms of thirteen weeks, and we have 5 periods of three quarters of an hour. It appears that we have $13 \times 3 \times 5 \times \frac{3}{4} = \frac{585}{4} \simeq 146$ teaching hours to cover the syllabus. In practice this is not so.

The first week of the Christmas term is usually spent with organizational tasks such as giving out books and materials and with the teacher revising previous work in an attempt to find out what the children already know. Depending on the organization of the school a certain amount of time will be spent on examinations. If examinations are held on the next to the last week of term (which is usually the case so that students can have their marks before they go on holiday), two weeks teaching time is lost. Our thirteen weeks term has become a ten week teaching term. Over the year a further two weeks is usually lost due to activities such as sports day, visits, day holidays, visiting speakers and so on.

A better estimate of our teaching time would be
$(10 \times 3 - 2) \times 5 \times \frac{3}{4} = 28 \times 5 \times \frac{3}{4} = 105$ hours.

Visit a local primary school – find out how much time is spent on the teaching of mathematics in a year.

When we know the total number of hours' time we have to cover the syllabus we study the syllabus and make a rough estimate of the time we can spend on each section. To consider year three as an example, in year three of the primary school the syllabus is as follows:

A. *Numeration*   1) whole numbers 2) fractions
B. *Basic operations*   1) addition and subtraction
 2) multiplication 3) division
C. *Measurement*   1) money 2) length 3) area
 4) volume 5) capacity 6) weight
 7) time
D. *Practical Descriptive Geometry* – as shown in detail on page 18.

Study the detailed syllabus for Primary III. Make some estimate of the time you think you will need to cover each section. *Visit a local primary school.* Find out from the Primary III teacher how much time he spends on each section of the syllabus.

Lesson titles

When we know the time we can spend on a particular topic we can begin to write a draft list of titles of lessons. Consider we find we have eight hours to cover the section on Practical Descriptive Geometry (see page 18 for details). We might decide to divide the topic into eight periods as shown below:

Period 1. Finding the properties of cubes and cuboids.
 2. Finding the properties of cylinders and spheres.
 3. Making models of cubes and cuboids a) with solid face b) skeleton.
 4. Drawing faces of cubes and cuboids on '2D' paper.
 5. Drawing '3D' pictures of cubes and cuboids.
 6. Making models of cylinders, studying faces of cylinder. Studying a sphere, slice a sphere.
 7. 'Fixing' the shape of a triangle. Drawing a triangle – sides and corners.
 8. The square corner – examples in '2D' and '3D'.

When we have carried out this process on each topic of the year's syllabus we can say we have organized our year's teaching. We have written a teacher's syllabus.

Exercises, Assignments and Projects
1 Write a teacher's syllabus in mathematics for one year of the primary school.
2 Visit a local primary school and discuss the syllabus you have produced in 1 with the teacher teaching that year.
3 Make a collection of primary school syllabuses.
4 Write a list of vocabulary a student will have to learn in studying the Descriptive Geometry in Primary III. See if you can write the meaning of each word in your list without reference to other books. Look up the words in a dictionary and compare these with your answers.

Chapter Three

Why Do We Teach Mathematics?

In our lesson plan we said we should think about the aim of a lesson. If we as teachers are not convinced of the aim and importance of our lesson how can we convince the children in our class to work hard and learn? Before we look at how we should think about the aims of a particular lesson let us consider general aims in the teaching of mathematics.

Mathematics of Life

The most obvious reason, to us, for teaching mathematics is that it is necessary for a person to have some knowledge of mathematics in order to live as a useful and effective member of the society.

A farmer requires knowledge of the processes of arithmetic to work out how much fertilizer to buy. A builder requires knowledge of shapes and solids, of measurement, etc. to design and build a house. We all require knowledge of the ordinary processes of arithmetic when we buy, by length, area or volume, at the market or visit the Post Office. We all require to have some knowledge of budgeting. If we have a job we must be able to work out our wage and personal tax. If we have a house we have to check water rate bills, perhaps electricity bills and so on. We may have a bank account or Post Office account. We may decide to buy a motor car or motor bicycle – can we afford it, what will it cost to maintain, what is the insurance and road tax for it, how much does it cost? We may wish to buy glass to fit a window or wood to fit a door – how do we know if we are buying the right size? Once we start working for other people, meeting other people, or travelling, we have to be able to tell the time. If we are travelling we have to be able to read timetables. If we are travelling by car we might like to estimate our time of arrival, so we must know what speed means.

We could fill several pages giving practical reasons why children should learn mathematics in school. And yet if you visit a primary school and ask the children is mathematics useful in their lives you will very often get the answer 'no'. In some respects this might be true as the children do not have bank accounts, etc. They are truthfully saying the mathematics they learn is not relevant to their present lives. In many cases, however, the reason why the children cannot see that mathematics is useful in their lives is that teachers often concentrate on teaching processes and 'tricks' in mathematics without giving any examples of how the process is useful in the child's present or future life. It is much easier to write 'what is $2 \times Sh9$?' rather than asking 'if a pencil cost Sh9 how much would two pencils cost?' In every lesson in mathematics a teacher should ask himself, 'How can I convince the children that the mathematics they are learning today is useful?' The answer very often will be 'by giving the children some practical questions or problems at the end of the lesson'. Occasionally you might be able to take the children to see mathematics in action – for example at the Post Office. Sometimes you may be able to get people who use mathematics in their job to come and talk about how they use mathematics in their lives.

As a general rule, practical word problems should appear in every lesson. Children find great difficulty in sorting out the mathematical processes required to solve word problems. The reason for this is that the children are rarely given examples of word problems in class. And yet in life the usual way we meet mathematics is through word problems.

Mathematics and Other Subjects

Mathematics is necessary in the study of most science subjects including geography. It is perhaps impossible to convince students of the necessity of learning mathematics so that they can better study other subjects in the future. We can, however, give examples of simple statistics and graphical presentations of information in our geography lessons at least to illustrate the use of mathematics in other subjects.

Other Aims in Teaching Mathematics

In Chapter One you were asked to discuss the statement 'it doesn't matter what subject we teach, but how we teach it'.

If this statement was wholly true for any subject in the school curricula then the subject should be removed from the school curricula. It is true that by teaching a subject in certain ways we can develop certain skills in the child. We should however make sure that the content taught is relevant.

When teaching we must be concerned with teaching relevant content but we should also be concerned with developing the child's mind so that he can solve problems for himself. At the end of the day what is important is what the children can do, not what we have 'taught'.

Here is a selection of aims for the primary mathematics teacher. Discuss them and see if you think that they are relevant for your teaching.

The aims of the primary mathematics teacher should be:
(a) to show the *pupils* how to observe accurately, and to recognize and record a variety of relationships between different quantities;
(b) to give the pupils practice in applying these relationships to different quantities such as money, area, length, etc.;
(c) to give the pupils practice in analysing a new problem and suggesting solutions;
(d) to develop the pupils' ability in recording information, whether it be graphical, three-dimensional pictures or in symbolic form, to help him in the understanding of relationships;
(e) to give the pupils practice in interpreting the information they have obtained and coming to conclusions from the information;
(f) to develop in the pupils a willingness to follow the teacher's explanation;
(g) to show the pupils that mathematics can be enjoyed.

The first 5 objectives are concerned with thinking and the last two with the attitude of the pupils.

A study of objectives in all subjects has been made by Bloom (*et al.*) which resulted in the publication of Bloom's Taxonomy. Bloom found that it was useful to divide objectives into two domains – the cognitive (thinking) domain and the affective domain. He divided the cognitive domain into six levels and the affective domain into five levels as follows:

Cognitive Domain

Knowledge	the ability to recall knowledge of specific facts, terminology conventions, trends and sequences, classification and categories, criteria, methodology, principles and generalizations, theories and structures.
Comprehension	the ability to make translations, interpretations and extrapolations.
Application	the ability to apply knowledge (which they must understand) in a new situation.
Analysis	the ability to analyse new situations, see relationships or organizational principles.
Synthesis	the ability to produce a new piece of communication, to propose a plan or set of operations or derive a set of abstract relations.
Evaluation	the ability to pass judgments in terms of the evidence available.

Affective domain

Receiving	to develop an awareness and a willingness to receive in the pupil.
Responding	to develop a willingness and satisfaction in response in the pupil.
Valuing	to develop an acceptance of a value or a commitment.

Organization
Characterization by a value or value complex.

Compare these objectives with those given on page 24 (a) to (e).

Let us discuss Bloom's taxonomy in relation to mathematics teaching.

Knowledge

This is self evident. Unless the child can recall the necessary knowledge and processes he will not be able to think in mathematics.

Comprehension

If the child has not understood a new concept he will not be able to apply it. Sometimes in mathematics it is not always clear that a child has fully understood a new concept as he applies a trick or formula hence obtaining the correct solution without understanding what he is doing. To be sure that a child has understood a concept, process, etc. a teacher should ask the child to explain how he has completed the task. If you are dealing with large classes at the 'top' end of the primary school, it is a good idea to ask the children to write in words what they have done in each step of, say, a calculation. For example, multiplication

```
 27
 ×6
 ---
162
 ---
```

Step I.   Multiply 7 units by 6.
          Answer 4 tens and 2 units (42).
Step II. Write down 2 in units column.
          Carry 4 tens.
Step III. Multiply 2 tens by 6.
          Answer 12 tens or 1 hundred and 2 tens.
          Add 4 from Step II = 1 hundred and 6 tens.
Step IV. Write down 6 in tens column and 1 in hundreds column.

You could ask the children to write or copy a detailed explanation of what they are doing for the first example of any new process. You will find they understand more quickly by doing this and they will find the explanation most useful when they are revising their work.

Application

Application requires little explanation, nor do you need convincing of its use. Most teachers use most of their mathematics time to give their children practice in application. You might like to discuss whether so much time should be spent this way. Often if a teacher spent a little more time on his explanations, or on allowing the children to reach their own conclusions, he would find that the children would require less practice in application.

Analysis, Synthesis and Evaluation

Many primary school teachers think that if they have shown their children how to apply mathematical principles and generalizations then they have achieved as much as they can. This might be true at the lower end of the primary school – and certainly even at the top of the primary school with some students. If however we use different teaching methods we can develop students' ability in these cognitive skills. For example we could take different sized circular objects, some strips of tape, rulers and razor blades into the classroom. We could ask the children to use the materials provided to find out the relationship between the radius and the circumference of a circle. We have directed their thoughts by supplying relevant materials but each child (or group of children) has to analyse the problem, suggest solutions to the problem, devise experiments to produce the results necessary to make conclusions, and finally make conclusions. We will discuss this in more detail when we consider methods of teaching in Chapter Five.

Affective Domain

Considering the affective domain should make us aware as teachers that we first of all have to get the children in a frame of mind to listen before we can start talking about their willingness to respond.

Many factors affect a child's willingness to listen and respond. Some children will respond to one teacher and not to another.

Here is a list of factors which can affect a child's willingness to respond. To what extent do you think each factor is important? Rewrite the list in the order of importance.

1. The health of the child (a) physically (b) emotionally.
2. The health of the teacher (a) physically (b) emotionally.
3. The attitude of the teacher to the child.
4. The attitude of the child to the teacher.
5. The physical conditions in the classroom (temperature, humidity, comfort of seating, materials available such as books, teaching aids, etc.).
6. The child's previous attainment and experience with the subject.
7. The time of day.

Can you think of other factors which will affect a child's willingness to learn?

Social training

It is understandable if you are thinking 'what has social training got to do with the mathematics teacher?'. Social training is the responsibility of the whole school. We want to send children from the school knowing what social standards are expected from them, how they are expected to behave, how to work harmoniously with other people, and so on.

Our classroom is an example of a group of people working together to produce a useful end product; it is a miniature society. How the children behave depends to a large extent on the teacher: is he fair, is he organized, is he consistent when dealing with discipline problems?

The teacher can devise smaller social groups within the classroom. For lessons in which the children do experiments he can divide them into groups of four. One child is to be the organizer or leader, one to be the secretary, one to be the experimenter and one to be the labourer. This simplifies organizational problems for the teacher. When equipment is given out it is the job of the labourer to collect the equipment – only one quarter of the class is allowed to move. The organizer must control his group and decide what is to be done; the secretary must produce four copies of the results (in the lower classes the teacher may have to produce work sheets on which the 'secretary' enters the results in the appropriate places). The success of the experiment depends on the accuracy with which the experimenter works; the tidiness of the classroom depends on the labourer. Each person has a certain responsibility; they know on what criteria they will be judged. The leader or organizer finds it is not always easy to be a leader – he has to learn to tell (ask) other children to do things in such a way that the other child does not resent the instruction, and so on.

After a few months the 'jobs' are reallocated: the labourer becomes the leader, the leader secretary, and so on. Each child has a chance of learning how to cope with the different position in the mini-society.

Exercises, Assignments and Projects

1 Visit a local primary school. Try and find out what percentage of children like mathematics. Find out why some children like mathematics and others do not.
2 Make a collection of train timetables, Post Office information booklets, building society and bank rates of interest, tax regulations, car insurance prices, etc., etc. Write to problems using the information you have collected. Keep your collection safely. You will find it useful when you start teaching.

3   Make a collection of general aims of mathematics teaching. Compare them with the aims discussed in this chapter.
4   Pick a mathematics topic. Write a list of objectives for the lesson you would produce on that topic. You can use the teachers' syllabuses shown in Chapter Two to help you.

Chapter Four

Teaching and Learning Aids

Teaching aids, as the name tells us, are aids which are used by the teacher to help him communicate his ideas. If an aid is produced for the children to find out something for themselves they are usually called learning aids.

If, in our teaching, we find it difficult to explain a concept so that the children understand we should look for an aid which will help us. Often, particularly for the less able child, the same point has to be repeated several times in order that the children understand. If this is the case we should look for several teaching aids so that we can repeat our point in different ways. Besides improving our ability to communicate ideas, aids add variety to our lessons which would perhaps otherwise be rather dull.

Some times we can buy teaching aids, but on the whole teaching aids made by the teacher are by far the best. A teaching aid made by the teacher is made to fit the particular situation in which the teacher finds himself. If a teacher has gone to the trouble to make a teaching aid he goes into the classroom with a different attitude, he has put thought into the lesson, he has decided what kind of aid he requires and has made the aid. He is not going to let all that thought and work go to waste.

In this chapter we will discuss teaching or learning aids by considering some examples of primary school mathematics topics and showing how aids can be used to help our ability to communicate the ideas.

Teaching Numbers 1 to 9

That sounds simple enough: we teach the children the meaning of number. But let us consider what the children have to learn.

The children have to learn the shapes of the different numbers, they have to learn the meaning of each number, they have to learn to recall the shape and meaning of the numbers when they are called by name, they have to learn to write the numbers, they have to learn to match each number to a group of different kinds of articles, they have to learn that there is an order of size, and they will be meeting words such as greater than, smaller than, and so on.

The children have a lot to learn before we can begin to think about teaching them simple addition and subtraction. If the children do not have a good concept of number they will find it impossible to understand addition or subtraction.

Most teachers would agree that you cannot teach numbers without using teaching aids. We require some form of counters whether they be seeds, bottle tops, beads or even larger objects such as bottles or bananas. We require wall charts showing the numbers and names together with the appropriate number of objects drawn. These objects should differ for each number – can you think why? We might use a sand tray so that the children can quickly trace out the shape of the number with their finger. We require the necessary implements for the children to learn to draw the numbers – some children will find it very difficult to hold a pencil and direct it to draw the shapes. We may have to give practice in using a pencil: following a maze, drawing patterns such as ℓℓℓℓℓ, ∧∧∧∧, and so on. We could make solid numbers from wood so that the children can hold them. We could make templates of numbers so that the children can draw around them.

We could continue for several pages giving a list of posible aids to teach numbers. In the exercises at the end of this chapter you will be asked to produce such a list.

Besides the kind of aids we use we are also concerned with how they are used. Two teachers could be given the same aids to use in their teaching; one teacher may fail to communicate the true concept and could confuse the children while the other teacher using the same materials could succeed.

Teacher I

The teacher places one bottle top on the desk and says, 'this is one bottle top'.

He places a further bottle top on the desk and says, 'there are two bottle tops'.

The teacher continues and will count one, two, and so on as he places the bottle tops on the desk.

Consider what the children should think.

'The teacher put one counter on the desk and said that is one counter. He placed another counter on the desk and said that was two counters. Ah, I understand the first one is called one and the second one is called two.'

```
   one      two      three
    •       • •      • • •
```

The children would not have the language to put this into words but the above is a logical conclusion which could be drawn from the way in which the aids were used by the teacher.

Teacher II

The second teacher places one counter on the desk and says, 'there is one counter on the desk'. He could draw this on the chalk board and show them how to write one.

```
      •       1       one
```

He then removes the counter from the desk. He then places two counters on the desk at the same time and says 'there are two counters on the desk'. He can draw this on the chalk board.

```
     • •      2       two
```

He would proceed in a similar manner for three. He finally places three groups on the table.

```
    •       • •      • • •
    1        2         3
```

The children cannot draw the wrong conclusion from this information.

When we have selected our teaching aids, we must think about how they must be used so that the children build the correct concept.

Note we are not saying that Teacher II is finished with teaching one, two and three. He will have to repeat this process several times using different objects so that the children realize that 'one' is not only connected to a counter. We can have one counter, one bottle top, one banana, etc.

The children could use the counters and be told to give three bottle tops to their neighbour, and so on.

We could produce wall charts so that the children are reminded of what they have learnt.

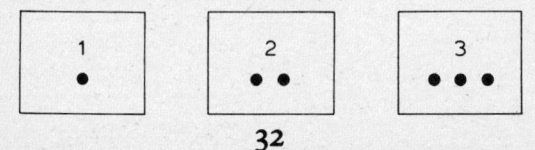

```
  ┌─────┐   ┌─────┐   ┌─────┐
  │  1  │   │  2  │   │  3  │
  │  •  │   │ • • │   │• • •│
  └─────┘   └─────┘   └─────┘
```

We could produce strips as shown below. The children could be asked to match the strips to the wall charts.

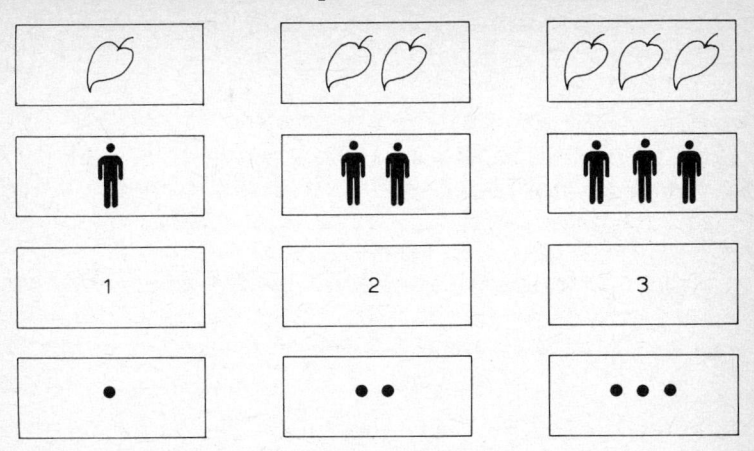

🌶	🌶 🌶	🌶 🌶 🌶
👤	👤 👤	👤 👤 👤
1	2	3
•	• •	• • •

We could use these strips to play games of recognition. The teacher lifts a strip and asks. How many spots are on the card? etc. The child who recognizes the meaning first takes the card so that he knows he has scored one point and so on. The strips could be shuffled and children asked to sort them into piles.

The children could be given a selection of the strips and could be asked to sort them in order of size.

We could use aids as shown below:

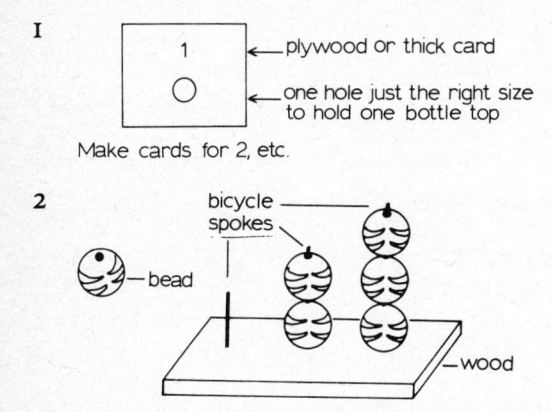

1

⟵ plywood or thick card
⟵ one hole just the right size to hold one bottle top

Make cards for 2, etc.

2

bicycle spokes
bead
wood

Cut bicycle spokes to size so that only one bead will fit on first, two beads on the second, and so on.

3   Make dominoes.

1	•• •

3	one

1	•• ••

•• ••	2

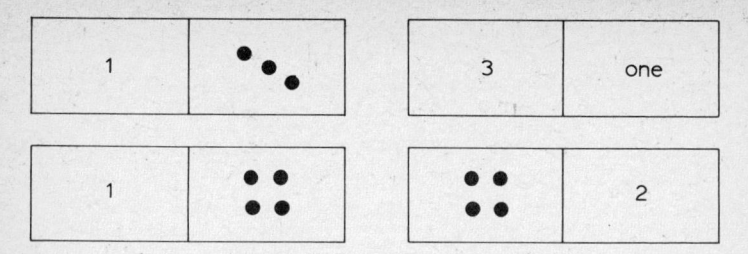

The children can play with the dominoes in the normal way or one child can be asked just to make a long line of dominoes matching as he goes along. Ask the child to make the line of dominoes as long as possible.

4   It is often useful to use money as counters as children have often heard their parents or brothers or sisters discussing how much things cost.

5   The teacher can produce materials for the children to use. Such as – join the dots:

$$1\;1\;2\;2$$

to help the children to learn to write their numbers.

6   Make matching strips. They can be made with jigsaw cuts and later with straight cuts.

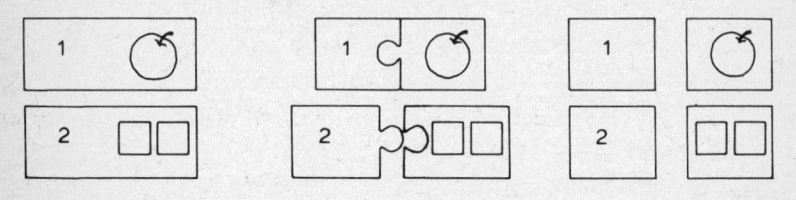

1	🍎
2	▢▢

1	🍎
2	▢▢

1	🍎
2	▢▢

and so on.

Let us now consider the teaching aids we could produce to teach place value.

Place Value

Another difficult concept to teach children is that the position in which we write a symbol is important.

It would be difficult or impossible to teach this concept without using teaching aids.

Let us consider the problem.

We have nine symbols.

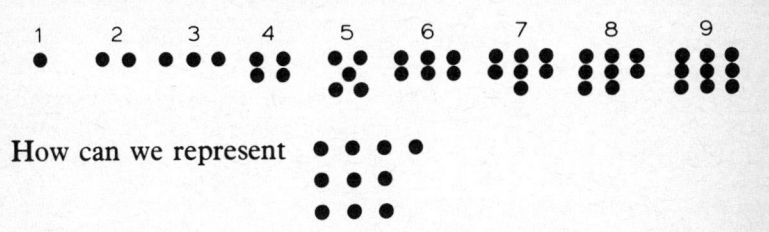

How can we represent [a 3×3 grid of dots]

We could invent another symbol – or we could say 'this is a big enough group to look at, let's call it one ten. To write it down we will make a new column':

Tens	Units
1	

We will write 1 in the tens column to represent [a 3×3 grid of dots]

or ● ● ● ● ● ● ● ● ● ●

A symbol written in the second column shows how many groups of ten we have.

A teaching aid which is often used to teach this idea is bundles of matches or straws, etc.

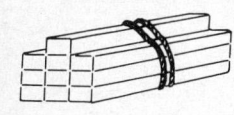

Once we have enough matches to make a bundle of ten we can tie them together and say we have one ten, etc.

Using this aid, a child has to count the matches to find if there are enough to make a bundle of ten.

Another aid we could use at this stage would be squares to represent the 'ones' and a rectangular prism to represent the 'tens' (made from wood or card). The children can then use a 'ten' as a measuring device to find out if they have enough 'ones' to make a 'ten'.

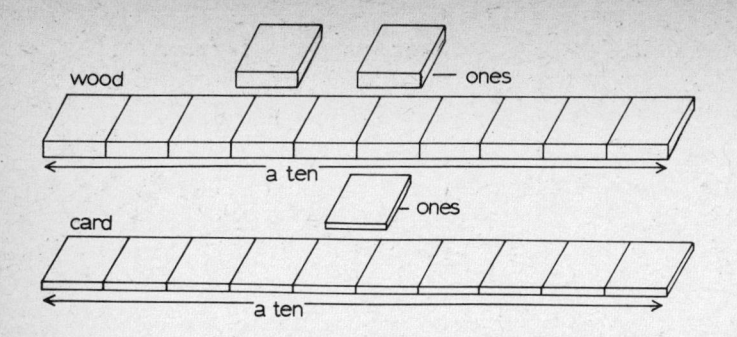

An easy way to make our wooden model is to cut thick bamboo into strips, longways:

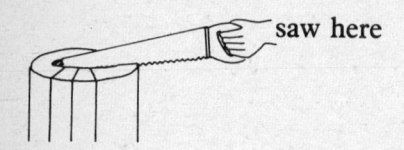

rub on sandpaper to make square, mark into tens.

Some strips can be cut to make our ones:

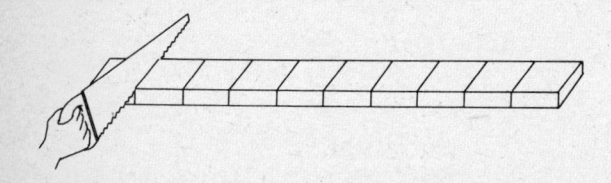

You may know a carpenter who can make you long strips of wood of cross section 1 cm × 1 cm, say. You can mark the wood every 10 cm. Cut some of the strips into 'tens' and some into 'ones'.

The children can use the aids as shown below:
Do this addition sum:

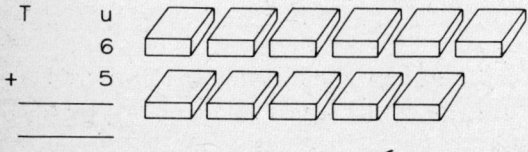

```
T   u
    6
+   5
———
```

The children place the units or 'ones' together in a line. They then place a 'ten' or measuring stick alongside to see if they can exchange one 'ten' for ten 'ones'.

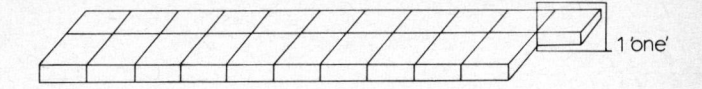

We have 1 'ten' and 1 'one' so we can write 1 in the tens column and 1 in the units column.

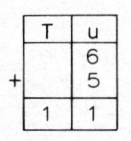

	T	u
		6
+		5
	1	1

All addition or subtraction sums should be laid out in column form for some time so that the children learn the meaning of place value.

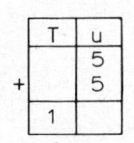

	T	u
		5
+		5
	1	

Tens should be written as 1 in the tens column and a space in the units column.

After some time zero should be introduced: the reason for having zero is so that we do not have to draw the columns all the time. Zero shows an empty column:

T	u
1	

can be written 10,

H	T	u
3		7

can be written 307.

To save children writing columns every time they do an addition or subtraction, we could duplicate sheets for them to use as shown.

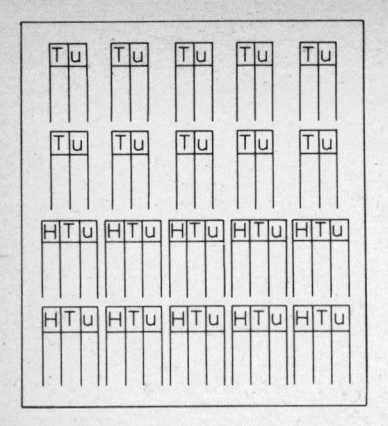

This will save time and will ensure that they do put the numbers in the correct columns. Children find difficulty in drawing the columns at right angles to the lines on the page.

A useful aid to use when teaching number bonds is the mathematical balance. This can be made as shown below:

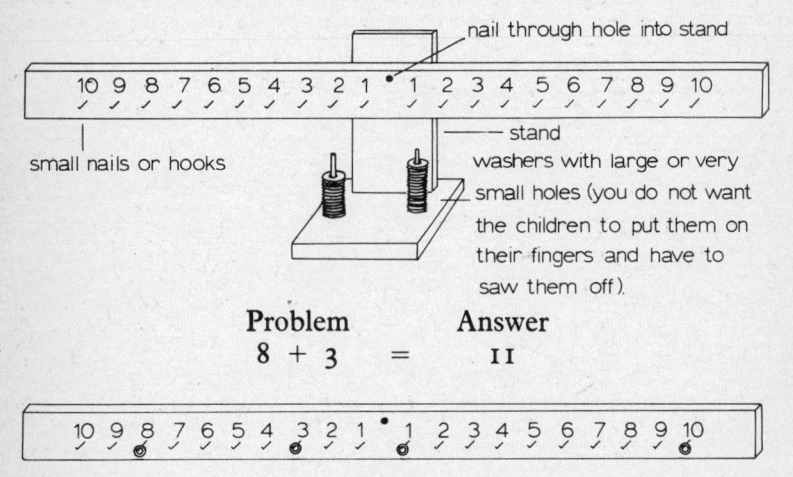

nail through hole into stand

small nails or hooks

stand

washers with large or very small holes (you do not want the children to put them on their fingers and have to saw them off).

Problem   Answer
8 + 3   =   11

Place washers on 8 and 3   Balance will be obtained when one washer is placed on 10 and one washer on 1.

An abacus is very useful when teaching place value. You can make one using wood, wire and some different coloured plastic beads as shown. Remember to put only 9 beads on each wire.

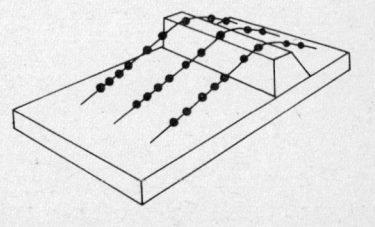

38

Fractions

When we introduce fractions we should use as many different shapes and shadings as possible.

If we make some simple teaching aids from strips of plywood or stiff card, the children can use them to do experiments to find out a great deal about fractions.

They can find equivalence in the same family

$\frac{1}{2} = \frac{2}{4} = \frac{4}{8}$; $\frac{2}{3} = \frac{4}{6} = \frac{8}{12}$

or equivalence in two different families

$\frac{1}{2} = \frac{3}{6}$; $\frac{3}{4} = \frac{9}{12}$

The children can use the strips to work out simple addition and subtraction problems involving fractions.

Paper folding can be usefully used to show what happens when we multiply fractions.

• The teacher folds the paper in half and says 'this is a half'. To find a half of a half the paper is folded again. We shade the half of a half and then open out the paper. The result is shown below:

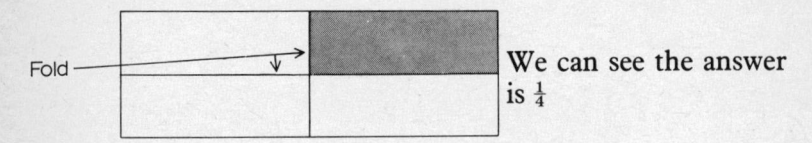

Fold

We can see the answer is $\frac{1}{4}$

Several examples are done and the results are entered in a table:

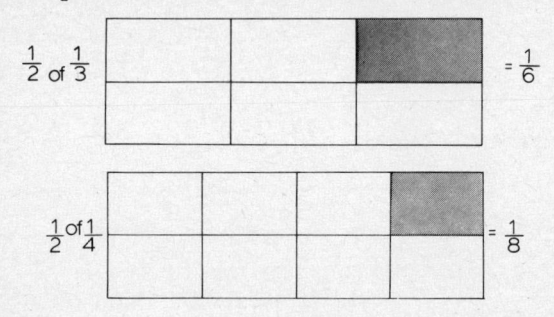

$\frac{1}{2}$ of $\frac{1}{3}$ = $\frac{1}{6}$

$\frac{1}{2}$ of $\frac{1}{4}$ = $\frac{1}{8}$

The children see that we can obtain the same result by multiplying numerators together and putting the answer over the denominators multiplied together.

By careful folding we can show how we reduce to the lowest terms.

$\frac{2}{3}$ of $\frac{3}{4}$

Fold the paper into four, take three parts; the fourth part is folded behind.

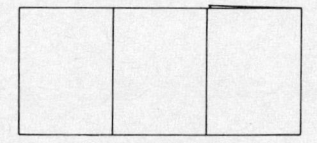

Now shade in $\frac{2}{3}$ of the three quarters and then unfold to see how much of the whole we have shaded.

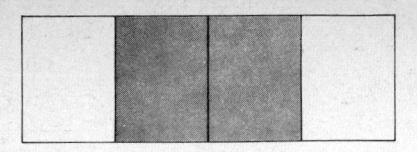

We have shaded $\frac{2}{4}$ or $\frac{1}{2}$

Try folding paper to solve other multiplication problems.

Many interesting aids can be made from paper; three dimensional cubes, rectangular prisms, etc. can be made using nets. They can be used when teaching the concept of volume.

Coloured paper is most useful to cut out shapes which can be pasted into a child's exercise book to help him make notes. An exercise book is often just a collection of spidery scrawls which have little or no meaning. An exercise book should be something worth looking at. The children should be encouraged to make notes on experiments they do. An exercise book should be useful when revising.

An example of how the exercise book could be used more usefully is shown below.

Area of a Triangle

Consider we are teaching the area of a triangle is half the base times the perpendicular height. The teacher could give the children two identical triangles, say A and B, as shown below:

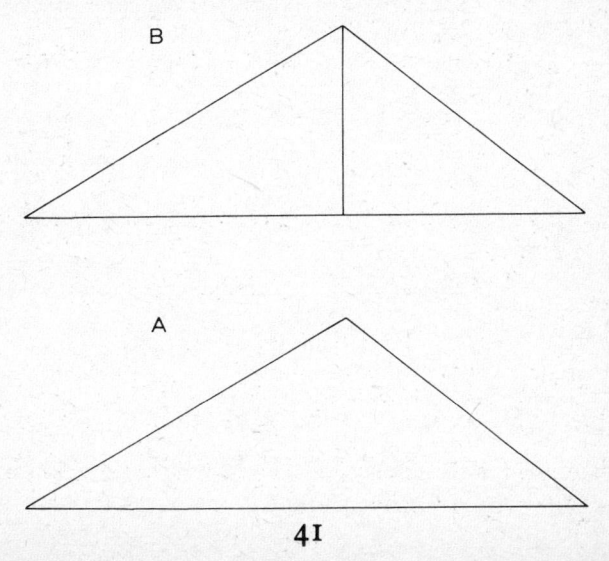

The children are asked to find the area of one triangle but are told they can use both triangles and can cut one triangle in two if they wish. With a broad hint like this, it doesn't take them long to discover that they cut the second triangle along the line already drawn on it and make a rectangle.

The children can use the triangles they were given to make notes in their exercise books. If the children were given two more triangles, the notes in their exercise books might look something like this. (The children stick the triangles in their books.)

To find the Area of a Triangle

We were given two triangles which were the same shape and size, as shown below. We were asked to find the area of one of the triangles

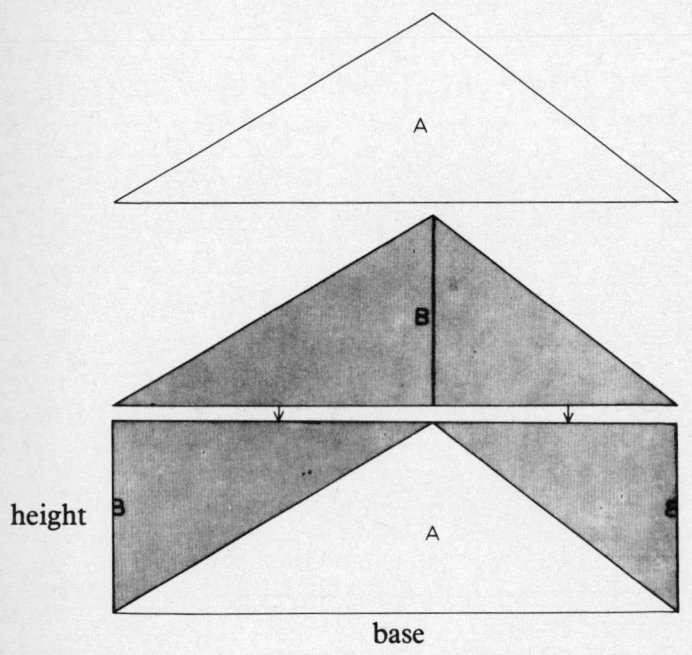

We cut one triangle into two pieces along the line shown in B above. We placed the pieces of the triangle B next to triangle A as shown below:

The whole area = base × height. The area of one triangle = half base times height as the area of the two triangles we were given

42

was equal. We know this because we put one triangle over the other and found it was the same area before we cut it into two.

We know now that to find the area of a triangle we measure the base and the height.

$$A = \tfrac{1}{2} bh$$

Exercises, Assignments and Projects

1. Visit a local primary school. Find out what aids they use to teach number. Look at Teaching Aids catalogues. Make a full illustrated list of the aids you could use to teach number. Say whether you would consider each aid as a teaching or a learning aid.
2. Study different primary mathematics books to see how they introduce number. Decide which book introduces number the best. Explain why and how you made your decision.
3. Make a mathematical balance. See if you can work out how it can be used to do subtraction, multiplication and division. The balance can be used to find remainders if we divide a number by another number which will not divide exactly. See if you can find out how this can be done.
4. Problems in addition and related skills should be made as attractive as possible by changing the method of presentation. They can be examples from their books. The children could make their own problems by using a dice, or a spinning top. Make a collection of interesting addition problems.
5. Pick a mathematics topic which you will be teaching. Find out what teaching aids you could buy to help you teach the topic. Find out what teaching aids you could make. Make the teaching aids and describe how you would use them in your teaching.
6. Draw nets from which you can make the following three dimensional teaching aids:
    (a) a centimetre cube
    (b) a rectangular prism
    (c) a triangular prism
    (d) a right pyramid.

Chapter Five

Different Methods of Teaching Mathematics

We have already mentioned, in Chapter One that there are an infinite number of methods in which a given lesson can be presented. In order that we can discuss methods in more detail we defined six 'methods' which span the spectrum of all methods. The methods were as follows:
1. the didactic or formal approach,
2. the formal demonstration,
3. teacher demonstration, class conclusion,
4. conducted class discussion,
5. conducted discovery, and
6. discovery methods.

In order to show how these different methods can be used in the classroom we will consider how the topic 'Pi' (π) could be 'taught' using the different methods. We will also discuss the objectives obtained by the different methods.

No matter which method of teaching is to be used a teacher has to follow certain steps.

He should (a) write down the title, (b) make sure he knows what the title means, (c) consider what knowledge he can assume and (d) consider how he is going to convince the children that the lesson is worthwhile.

Writing down the title is easy: 'Pi' – but what does it mean? You may find the answer in a dictionary. You should encourage the children in your class to look up words they do not understand in mathematics in the dictionary.

If the circumferences and diameters of different circles are measured and the ratio of the circumference to diameter for each circle is found, the same number is obtained (i.e. the ratio is constant). This constant is given the name Pi (π). π is the constant ratio between the circumference and diameter of a circle.

We are now clear what the children have to learn. What knowledge can we assume?

As we are talking about a hypothetical case this is impossible to say. But if we are teaching this topic in primary V, as recommended by the Federal Ministry of Education's Primary Mathematics Curriculum, we can assume:
(a) the children know the meaning of a circle,
(b) they know circles vary in size,
(c) they know the meaning of perimeter, diameter, radius and circumference,
(d) they can draw circles using circular objects to draw around,
(e) they can measure with some degree of accuracy,
(f) they have some knowledge of equations.

The teacher should then consider the introduction to the lesson. Why should we want to know about π? Before you read on try and see if you can think of how you could convince a primary V child that it is interesting to learn about π.

Perhaps problems like these may catch their interest.

If a man wishes to make a bucket of diameter 24 cm and is using wire to strengthen the top, can he calculate what length of wire he requires?

If we measure the diameter of a bicycle wheel, can we calculate how far the bicycle will travel after one rotation of the wheel?

We could perhaps explain that π will be used in their future study of mathematics to find area and volume of cylindrical objects.

It is not necessary to introduce every new topic by trying to convince the children it is of practical use as children can get tired of seeing everything has a practical use. The introduction may just be a few words. It is however worth considering local practical uses of the content of a lesson as it will help you to write some interesting problems for the application session at the conclusion of your lesson.

From this point our preparation of the lesson will change depending on the method of teaching we use.

The Didactic or Formal Approach

The teacher might start his lesson by questioning the children on the knowledge assumed.

As he obtains answers he would make a summary on the chalkboard. He may draw a diagram showing the diameter, radius and circumference of the circle. He would then give his introduction to the lesson.

He could then draw circles of different sizes on the chalkboard (perhaps in order of size) and ask the children what happens to the length of the circumference as the diameter increases in size. (He would expect the answer that as the length of the diameter increases the length of the circumference increases.)

The teacher would then tell the class that it has been found that if the diameter of a circle is doubled or trebled, for example, the circumference is found to double or treble, but the ratio of 'C' to 'd' always remains the same.

$$\frac{C}{d} = \pi \text{ (pi)}$$

$$\pi = \frac{22}{7} \text{ or approximately 3.}$$

The teacher might then demonstrate how to use the formula to find 'C' knowing 'd', and 'd' knowing 'C'. The teaching aids used were the chalkboard and a board compass.

The teacher then gives the children some problems to do in their books – he walks around the class dealing with children's difficulties.

We will discuss the objectives achieved later.

Formal Demonstration

The title, meaning and knowledge assumed will be as before. The teaching aids will include several tin cans of different diameter, sticking tape and razor blades or string and scissors, a rubber and two hard-backed books and a large sheet of drawing paper.

The teacher might start his lesson as before – with questions on the assumed knowledge – building up a summary on the chalkboard as he receives answers, and giving his introduction.

He would then, perhaps, draw some circles of differing size on the board and ask the children what happens to the length of the circumference as the diameter gets larger.

After obtaining replies from the class he would say that he would carry out an experiment to find out if there was a connection or relationship between the length of the diameter and the circumference.

He would draw around the base of each tin forming a circle on the drawing sheet and number the tins and circles. He could measure the diameter of each circle drawn on the drawing sheet. Or he could use the two books, as shown in the illustration on the right, and a ruler, to measure the diameter.

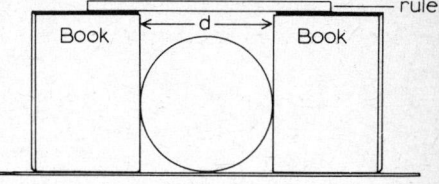

Fig. 5.1

To measure the circumference he could wrap the sticky tape around the tins so that it completely surrounds the tin and overlaps. He would then cut through the double tape with the razor. On peeling off this tape he will have a length of tape equal to the circumference of the tin. He can stick this tape next to the drawing of the circle on his drawing sheet and measure its length. As he repeats the process for other tins he could build up a wall chart as illustrated in figure 5.2.

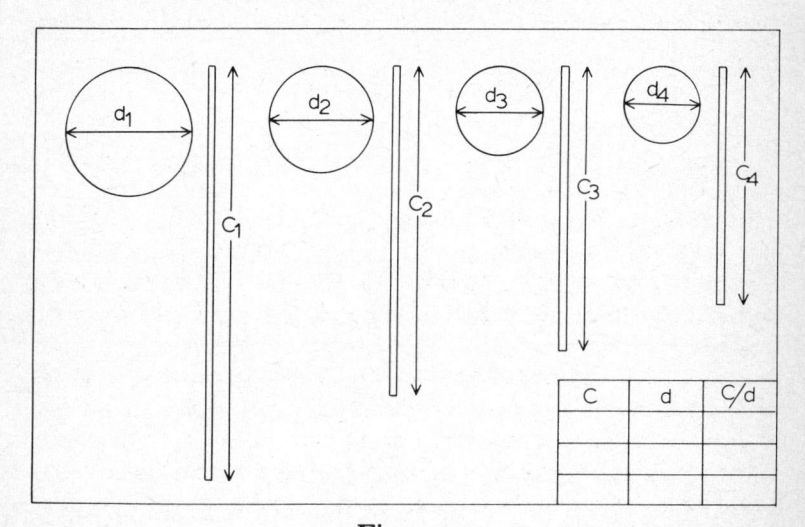

Fig. 5.2

He then proceeds to calculate $\frac{C}{d}$ for each case showing that he obtains (within experimental error) the same number each time. He explains the conclusion to the children.

He could then proceed as before, giving the children problems and checking their ability to do them.

Teacher Demonstration, Class Conclusion

This lesson would proceed as the previous method up to the point where the results were obtained.

The children would then be given the obtained values of 'C' and 'd'. They would be asked to explain the experiment carried out and be asked to see if they can find a connection between 'C' and 'd'.

After the children have written down their conclusion a class discussion would be held at the end of which a final conclusion would be reached. The children would then express their conclusions in the most clear and precise terms and then be given practice in applying the conclusion.

Conducted Class Discussion

In this method the children are involved earlier in the lesson. The summary of previously obtained knowledge and introduction would be the same as in the *Formal Demonstration* method. After that stage the problem is given to the class. How can we find out if there is a relationship or connection between the size of the circumference and the diameter of a circle?

This method is sometimes called the questioning method. The teacher collects ideas from the children but has often to keep the class thinking by asking another question and yet another. The teacher must listen carefully to the idea put forward by the child. If it is not complete he should think of a question he can ask which might help the child further the idea.

A child might say 'We measure the diameter and circumference'. The teacher says, 'Good – how can we measure the diameter?' The answer from some child might be, 'Draw around the tin and measure the diameter of the drawn circle'. The teacher could question the accuracy: 'Will the circle we have drawn be equal in diameter to the diameter of the tin?' The thickness of the pencil lead and how near we keep the lead to the edge of the tin, and so on, could be discussed. The diameter is the distance through the centre – do we know where the centre of the circle is? The diameter is the largest distance across the circle – are we sure we are measuring the diameter? The teacher might ask, 'Could we use the two hardbacked books (or two blocks of wood, etc.) to help us measure the diameter?'

The teacher would then lead a discussion on how we measure the circumference in a similar way. If different methods are suggested the teacher could try them all and see which is the best. When thirty five (or more) interested minds tackle a problem you will be surprised how many ideas emerge.

The teacher would then lead a discussion on how to deal with the results and make a table.

We could try $C - d$, $C + d$, $\frac{C}{d}$, $\frac{d}{C}$, $C \times d$.

We could stick our tapes, used to measure the circumference, on a scale showing the diameter as shown in figure 5.3.

The teacher would still be doing all the practical work – but following the suggestions put forward by the children.

The children would again be given the results and be asked to come to their own conclusions. Finally as in the previous method a final class discussion would take place on 'what we have found out'.

Many teachers shy away from this method as they think once you give a class permission to put forward their ideas then the class degenerates into noise. This of course can happen if the teacher has not come well prepared with materials with which to carry out the children's suggestions and he has to go looking for things.

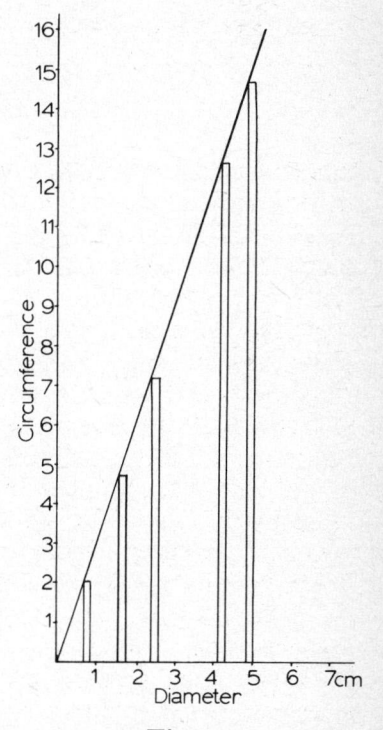

Fig. 5.3

It can also happen if the teacher has not insisted previously that children come to the classroom to work and that they behave with good manners – not talking all together and so on. If a teacher insists on not wasting time and on good manners in the classroom he will find he has no discipline problems.

Perhaps it would be a mistake to use this method with a new class or at the start of teaching practice. You must feel confident you are in control of the situation to lead an efficient discussion class.

Conducted Discovery

In this method even more of the activity of the lesson is passed to the children. The teacher introduces the lesson, revises necessary previous knowledge, discusses the problem with the children and accepts ideas for the solution. He then supplies the necessary materials for the children to carry out their investigations (different children, or groups of children, may have suggested different ways of finding out the solution so may require different materials). After the children have completed their own investigations and drawn their own conclusions a class discussion takes place to reach final conclusions. The children are then given problems on which to apply their new-found knowledge.

Discovery Approach

In the discovery approach the teacher waits until each child proposes the problem and then discusses with the child how he can solve the problem. This does not mean that the teacher sits there waiting for the child to think of the problem. For the discovery approach to be used successfully the teacher must turn his classroom into a source of stimuli to problems. He will use the walls of the classroom to full effect, cutting out illustrations from magazines, etc. and writing questions such as 'How can we find the circumference of a circle?'. The main idea behind the discovery approach is that if the child proposes the problem for himself, he will apply himself to the solution with more energy and enthusiasm. The teacher must keep cupboards full of coloured paper, measuring devices, watches, card, weighing scales, tins, etc. so that he has material available for the children to investigate some problem. The teacher must keep records of each child's progress as each child will be at a different place on the syllabus. The teacher must be able to keep his eye on many different activities going on at the same time in his classroom and make sure the children are not wasting time.

Before reading the rest of the chapter look over the different methods again, with the following questions in your mind. Which method do you think is the best? Do you think the same method will be the best in all circumstances?

Discussion of Methods of Teaching

Let us consider the objectives achieved by the different methods illustrated above.

In the *didactic* approach, the teacher has done all the thinking for the children. He has analysed the problem before the lesson and produced a logical sequence of communications. He has drawn the conclusions. The children have learnt that $\frac{C}{d} = \pi$ and have applied the new 'trick' to some problems.

In the *formal demonstration* approach the children should be more interested and willing to learn as they enjoy watching the teacher carry out an experiment. Aids have been used and a certain amount of repetition has been built into the lesson. The children have been convinced of the truth of the statement and have applied their new-found knowledge. The children have not had any exercise in the higher cognitive skills.

In the *class discussion* method we increase the involvement of the class by asking them to draw the conclusion separately. Each child has to analyse the results, to draw a conclusion and has to put together (synthesize) a piece of communication which explains his conclusion. We have allowed the children to exercise more cognitive skills.

As we progress through the other methods to the discovery method, the children have a greater opportunity to exercise these skills as well as having practice in practical skills such as cutting out, folding, measuring angles and writing up results.

It would appear then that the *conducted discovery* or *discovery* methods should be used as often as possible. This would seem a logical conclusion as these methods obtain more objectives. There are, however, many more things we should consider.

When a teacher gives his first lesson he has many things to think about. He is concerned with getting to know the children, learning how to look at children so that he can see if they understand, overcoming his own shyness at standing in front of 30–40 pairs of eyes. The teacher has to develop skill in using the chalkboard, skills in questioning, in organization and keeping the children's minds on the subject matter of the lesson.

Keeping control of a class discussion so that the children keep on the point and do not get out of hand has to be learnt by the teacher. Before a teacher allows children to do experiments on their own, he must be confident that the class concerned respects him and will apply themselves to the experiments seriously. Children need convincing that they can think usefully for themselves. If children have been taught by formal methods all their lives and the next day a teacher changes to conducted discovery methods, the children will be lost. They will decide this method is a waste of time: 'Why don't you just tell us the correct answer?'

The correct method to use therefore will depend on the previous experiences of the teacher, the content to be communicated, and the children.

Most tutors would recommend that student teachers and teachers in their first year's teaching should not attempt the conducted discovery or the discovery methods. After a teacher has taught through the year's work he will have a firm understanding of the work to be covered in a year. He will have a collection of teaching aids which he can then use in the same lesson for different children. To prepare for a discovery approach lesson from 'scratch' requires a great deal of work. Unless the teacher is willing to do this work properly, the lesson will fail. Unless the class has been taught by the discovery approach before, the new teacher should not attempt this method until he has had some experience and feels confident that he can control situations which are always changing.

If a teacher decides to start using the discovery approach, he should slowly change his method of teaching. He should, for example, teach by the second method for a week and then the third method for a week and so on. He should slowly get the children used to the idea that they are going to be more involved in the lesson. He should show them that they can think things out for themselves with the teacher's guidance.

The names for the different methods have been devised to help our discussion. In practice several methods can be used in the same lesson – a teacher could give a lesson part of which uses the formal approach and part of which could be the conducted discovery approach. The teacher could organize a lesson without speaking by using a card system. The children could work through cards which lead them through a certain thought process. If this method is used, each child could progress at his own pace. An example of a work card for a lesson on the sum of the three angles of a triangle is shown below:

Angles in a triangle
Draw a large triangle on a piece of card. Cut out the triangle.

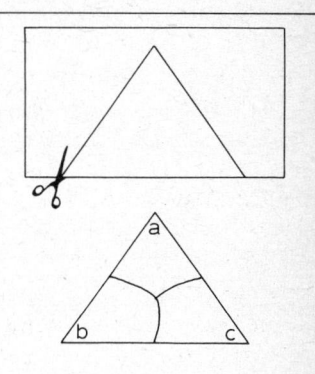

Label the angles of the triangle. Cut the triangle into three pieces as shown on the right.

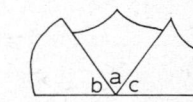

Place the three angles of the triangle together. What conclusion can you draw?

Besides using different methods of teaching, a teacher can organize his class in different ways. If he finds that his children have wide differences in mathematical ability he may decide to split the children into three groups. He may decide to treat these groups as separate 'classes', giving work to the other two groups while 'teaching' the third group. He may decide that the 'bright group' doesn't need much of his attention. They can learn on their own from their books or from a work card system.

The teacher may decide to organize leaders for groups of children for periods when the children are applying their new knowledge on problems. If a child is having difficulty with a problem he first of all asks his 'leader' if he can help. If the leader can help he does so. If the leader cannot help the leader and the child who has the difficulty ask the teacher to explain.

Variety

We have seen from our discussion on methods that there is an infinite number of ways of teaching. If we go into most schools we find that a teacher has decided on one approach and 'sticks to it' for every lesson. The children know the pattern of the school time table – it is usually exactly the same in each class throughout the primary school and exactly the same each day of the week. The children know the pattern a lesson takes: teacher talks – class do some work – bell goes. Can we really hope to produce a willingness to learn in the students by such organization and methods?

Variety is the spice of life – or so it is said. A teacher should not stick to one method of teaching – if he does he will soon become bored. He should try different methods and use different methods of organization. Here are some questions for you to think about.

Is it necessary that the children's desks should stay in exactly the same pattern in the classroom for the whole year?

Is it necessary or even desirable that all mathematics lessons should take place in the classroom?

Exercises, Projects and Assignments

1. Choose a mathematics topic from the primary school syllabus. Show how you would teach the topic using (a) the 'formal' approach and (b) the 'conducted discovery' approach.
2. In most classes in which we teach we will find there is a wide range of 'mathematical ability'. Discuss how you would organize the subject matter and your teaching methods to take account of this.
3. Visit different primary schools in your area. Find out what methods of teaching are used.
4. Study a work card system.
5. Prepare a work card system for a primary mathematics topic of your choice.
6. Write an essay discussing the relative merits of the different methods of teaching discussed in this chapter.

Chapter Six

Examples of Lessons Prepared in Some Detail for Different Ages

In the previous chapters we have discussed objectives and methods in a general way. We have now to apply these generalizations, in preparing lessons. We may have to adapt some of the generalizations (or even ignore them) depending which age range we are teaching; for example, can children make their own notes at different stages of the primary school?

In this chapter you are given examples of lessons prepared for different age ranges. The age range is stated in each case. Study the different lessons critically. Write a critique on each lesson plan. Make your critique constructive, not destructive. If you think there is something wrong with the lesson plan explain what you think is wrong and what you would do instead. If you can find nothing to criticize you have not really thought about the lesson enough.

Primary 1   Fractions
Objective   That the children should be able to identify $\frac{1}{2}$ and $\frac{1}{4}$ using concrete objects and shapes and will be able to write $\frac{1}{2}$ and $\frac{1}{4}$.
Knowledge assumed   The children can write and know the meaning of numbers 1, 2 and 4. Most children will have met the word 'half' – half way there, half a banana, and so on.
Teaching aids   Oranges, card, duplicated shapes, squared paper, etc.
Procedure   The children cannot discover how to write a half or a quarter. In consequence the method which will be used will be 'teacher demonstration, class discussion'.

We introduce the lesson with a discussion on the word a 'half': does anyone know what it means? Can anyone give examples of it being used?

The teacher can write the examples on the chalk board:
          half way to school
          half way home
          half an orange   and so on.

The teacher could give an orange to a child and ask the child to cut the orange in such a way that he can take half the orange and give half to another child. The teacher asks the child to explain what he has done. 'The orange is cut into two parts'.

Can the child explain anything about the two parts? – 'The two parts are equal in size.' 'The orange has been cut into two equal parts.'

Another child might be given another orange. The teacher asks the child to take half of the orange and explain what he is doing.

'I must cut the orange into two equal parts and then take one part.'

This form of questioning can be repeated with many different concrete objects until the teacher is sure the children know that 'a half of any concrete object means one part of the object is taken after the object has been divided into two pieces'. The teacher could finish the first period by asking the children what he would have to do to take half a cardboard square, circle or rectangle.

In the next period the teacher would start his lesson by revising the previous lesson.

He could see if the children could carry out instructions such as, 'take half of a sheet of paper'. 'Place the chair half way between the desk and the window.'

He could see if the children could transfer the idea to a collection of objects. 'Take half of a pile of seeds (or bottle tops).'

When the teacher is sure the children know the meaning of 'a half' he could explain how we write one half using mathematical symbols.

$\dfrac{1}{2}$ ← tells us how many parts to take

the bottom number tells us how many equal parts the whole apple (banana) is divided into.

The children should be given many examples of single objects and groups of objects and asked to find half.

$\frac{1}{2}$ of the objects

Diagrams showing examples of what the children do should be placed on the classroom wall.

Children should be given practice in writing the symbol $\frac{1}{2}$. Many children will find difficulty in writing $\frac{1}{2}$. Teachers agree that children have to learn to write a, b, c, but when teaching mathematics they assume children can write $\frac{1}{2}, \pi, \alpha$ without any practice at all.

The children should be given pictures of squares and circles and asked to shade in $\frac{1}{2}$ the picture. The 'square' could be drawn on squared paper so that the children can produce patterns when shading a $\frac{1}{2}$ of the square.

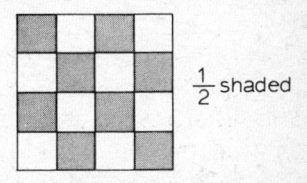

$\frac{1}{2}$ shaded

The teacher will then follow a similar pattern of lessons to teach the meaning of $\frac{1}{4}, \frac{2}{4},$ and $\frac{3}{4}$.

Some children will appreciate that a half of a half is $\frac{1}{4}$; this might be noted but not expected.

We would, however, expect the children to know that $\frac{1}{4}$ is smaller than $\frac{1}{2}$,
$\frac{1}{2}$ is greater than $\frac{1}{4}$, and
$\frac{3}{4}$ is greater than $\frac{1}{2}$, etc.

Primary 2   Addition of two digit numbers
Objectives   (a) To give further practice in addition of two digit numbers without exchanging or 'renaming'.
(b) To do addition of two digit (and then three digit) numbers with exchanging or renaming (in vertical and horizontal arrangement).

Knowledge assumed
(a) The children know the meaning of and can 'read' and write numbers up to 100.
(b) The children can add two digit numbers with sum not greater than 40 without exchanging or renaming.

Teaching aids   Single matches and bundles of ten, single unit coins and 10 unit coins, 1 cm^3 pieces of wood, 10 cm × 1 cm × 1 cm pieces of wood.

Procedure
Revise meaning of columns.

T	u
1 1	9

written 19
written 10
etc.

19 means 1 ten and 9 units
Test number bonds to 10.

Show 2+3 = 3+2

+	0	1	2	3	4	5	6	7	8	9
0	0	1	2	3	4	5	6	7	8	9
1	1	2	3	4	5	6	7	8	9	10
2	2	3	4	5	6	7	8	9	10	
3	3	4	5	6	7	8	9	10		
4	4	5	6	7	8	9	10			
5	5	6	7	8	9	10				
6	6	7	8	9	10					
7	7	8	9	10						
8	8	9	10							
9	9	10								
10	10									

Test ability to add without exchanging or renaming in vertical and horizontal arrangements.

E.g. 12 + 13 = ☐ ,   T u   T u
                     3 4   1 6
                    +2 5   +1 2
                    ────   ────

Do several examples of addition with exchanging or carrying. Use aids to show the meaning of the number carried.

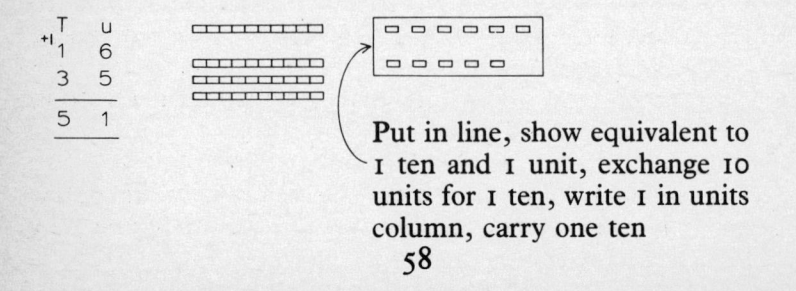

 T u
+1
 1 6
 3 5
 ────
 5 1

Put in line, show equivalent to 1 ten and 1 unit, exchange 10 units for 1 ten, write 1 in units column, carry one ten

58

Give the children examples to do. Ask them to use the aids provided.

Give examples in vertical arrangement.

After the children have had some experience doing examples with aids, ask them to do problems without aids but explaining what they are doing, e.g.

```
 T  u
 4  5     4 tens and 5 units, add 2 tens and 8 units.
+2  8     Answer 6 tens and 13 units
―――――     or  6 tens, 1 ten and 3 units
 7  3     or  7 tens and 3 units.
```

Give exercise to be done without aids or explanation.
Show different ways in which addition can be done.

5 + 8 = 8 + 5 = 13
5 + 8 = 5 + 5 + 3 = 13
5 + 8 = 3 + 2 + 8 = 13
5 + 8 = 5 − 2 + 10 = 13

Primary 3   Multiplication
Objectives (a) to give further practice in using multiplication facts from 1 × 1 to 10 × 10,
(b) to multiply two digit numbers by one digit number,
(c) to multiply three numbers taking two at a time.

Knowledge assumed That the children know how to find the answers to multiplication problems using the method of repeated addition.

The children know the multiplication sign (×).
The children read 2 × 3 as two groups (or sets) of 3.
The children know 2 × 3 = 3 × 2 = 6.
The children know their multiplication tables for 2 and 3.

Teaching aids Counters, number spinning tops, number dice, games involving multiplication, flash cards, hundred square charts, magic squares, number lines, kobo coins, 10 kobo coins, Naira (or matches or wood strips), squared paper, among others.

Procedure The children should be able to give multiplication facts readily and quickly. In order to do this the children should be given time to build up their own set of tables, to use them in various enjoyable activities and finally to learn them *by heart*. The 'tables' will be used in practical problems concerning money, length, area, weight and time, during the third year. Time spent on ensuring the children know their multiplication facts ensures that time is not wasted continually returning to 'repeated addition'.

As this 'lesson' will cover several weeks of class periods it is impossible to explain in detail what could take place in each period. The outline below should give some ideas on which you can build.

Procedure

Give an oral test to revise the multiplication tables for 2 and 3.

Revise multiplication sign; 2×3 reads – two groups of three and $2 \times 3 = 3 \times 2$.

Get the children to build the multiplication tables for 4 writing their results as shown below.

○
○
○   = one group of $4 = 1 \times 4 = 4 = 4 \times 1 =$ four ○○○○
○   groups of 1

○○○
○○○
○○○ = three groups of $4 = 3 \times 4 = 12 = 4 \times 3 =$ ○○○○
○○○   four groups of 3   ○○○○
                                                           ○○○○
                                                           ○○○○

etc.

Write the multiplication sum on one side of a flash card and the answer on the back.

The children can use the flash cards in pairs. One child holds up the flash card, the second child has to give an answer.

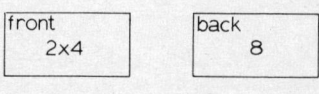

front		back
2x4		8

If the answer is correct the child takes the card. This game can be repeated several times on different days until the child 'wins' all the cards.

Give practice in answering questions such as $4 \times 8 =$ ☐

Give practice in answering questions in the written form such as:

If there are five tomatoes in each pile of tomatoes and we take six piles, how many tomatoes do we have?

Get the children to build multiplication tables for 5 using 10 unit coins and one unit coins. Then proceed as above.

Get the children to build multiplication tables for 6 using the number line.

| 1 2 3 4 5 6 7 8 9 10 11 12 13 14 15 16 17 18 19 20 |

Proceed as for 4 times tables.

Get the children to build multiplication tables for 7 using 1g and 10g weights, and so on.

We have changed the aid used in each case (a) for variety and (b) so that the children appreciate that the abstract number can refer to different objects.

As more tables are built up the flash cards are mixed with the previous set. The flash card game can become quite exciting.

Get the children to record all their results on one chart, which we could call the magic square, as shown below.

x	1	2	3	4	5	6	7	8	9	10
1										
2								16		
3										
4										
5					25					
6										
7										
8										
9			27							
10										

Some examples have been filled in.

If you can duplicate several blank magic squares, holes can be cut in blanks. When these are placed over the magic square the answer is revealed.

The children can answer many interesting questions using their magic squares, such as:

When we multiply an even number by an even number the answer is always an —— number.

When we multiply an odd number by an odd number the answer is always an —— number; and so on.

1	2	3	4	5	6	7	8	9	10
11	12	13	14	15	16	17	18	19	20
21	22	23	24	25	26	27	28	29	30
31	32	33	34	35	36	37	38	39	40
41	42	43	44	45	46	47	48	49	50
51	52	53	54	55	56	57	58	59	60
61	62	63	64	65	66	67	68	69	70
71	72	73	74	75	76	77	78	79	80
81	82	83	84	85	86	87	88	89	90
91	92	93	94	95	96	97	98	99	100

Produce 100 squares using the ink duplicating machine. Ask the school secretary to type several on a master sheet for you. The children can shade multiples of say 7 and so on. They could be asked to shade multiples of 2 in one colour and multiples of 4 in another. Ask them what they notice about the pattern.

Do you think a hundreds square could be used to teach the lowest common multiple (L.C.M.)?

Look at different textbooks; see if you can find some interesting problems. All the children in your class will no doubt have the same mathematics text. The teacher, however, should have a collection of different texts so that he can vary the type of questions or give a child who requires additional practice some new problems. Children rarely learn from going over problems at which they have already failed. Study different text books to see if they give you any more ideas on how to *teach* 'tables'.

Primary 4   L.C.M.

The lowest common multiple of two numbers is the smallest number which can be divided by the given two numbers separately, without leaving a remainder.

The lowest common multiple must be equal to or greater than the larger of the two given numbers.

Because the answer, in most cases, is larger than the given numbers many children become confused between L.C.M. and the highest common factor (H.C.F.). It is therefore suggested that L.C.M. and H.C.F. are not taught close together.

It is necessary to be able to find the L.C.M. of a group or set of numbers in order that we can add fractions. In practice in life situations we use $\frac{1}{2}, \frac{1}{3}, \frac{1}{4}, \frac{1}{5}, \frac{1}{6}, \frac{1}{8}, \frac{1}{10}$, and $\frac{1}{12}$'s. The children should be shown how to find the lowest common multiple of sets of two or three of the numbers in the numerators of these fractions.

Knowledge assumed

The children know what is meant by (a) a factor, (b) a prime factor and (c) a multiple of a number.

Procedure

Revise the meaning of the terms in 'knowledge assumed'.

Explain to the children that they will be given sets of two numbers and they will be required to find the common multiples of the two numbers up to a certain number. If you have duplicated several '100 squares' you could ask them to shade in yellow all multiples of 2 and in green all multiples of 3.

The children will find the following squares have been shaded in in both colours – 6, 12, 18, 24, 30 etc. All these numbers are common multiples of 2 and 3.

The smallest or 'lowest' multiples of 2 and 3 which is common to both 2 and 3 is 6. 6 is said to be the lowest common multiple of 2 and 3.

Give the children further examples to work out for themselves. They can either use 100 squares as above or write the numbers as shown below.

Multiples of 2:   2, 4, **6**, 8, 10, **12**, 14, 16, **18**, 20, 22, **24**, 26
Multiples of 3:   3, **6**, 9, **12**, 15, **18**, 21, **24**,

common multiples
lowest common multiple

Ask the children to label the common multiples and the lowest common multiple so that they become used to using the words correctly.

Repeat with other pairs of numbers.

Repeat with sets of three numbers as in the example below.

Multiples of 3 – 3, 6, 9, **12**, 15, 18, 21, **24**, 27, 30, 33, **36**, 39
Multiples of 4 –   4, 8, **12**,   16, 20,   **24**,   28, 32,   **36**,   40
Multiples of 6 –   6, **12**,   18,   **24**,   30,   **36**,

common multiples   lowest common multiple

Use the squared paper and ask the children to draw a number line as shown below. Shade the multiples of each number. Ask questions for the children to solve such as: Use your number line to find the L.C.M. of 2, 4, and 5; 2, 3, 4, and 6, and so on.

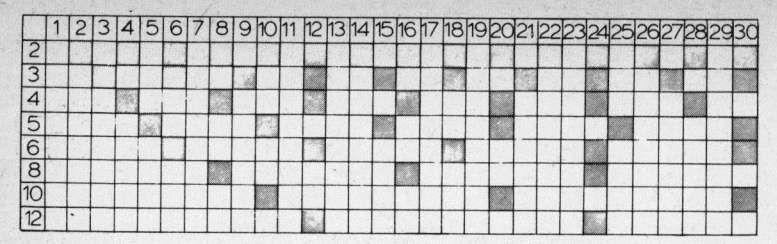

Ask the children to write the set of numbers as prime numbers and to write the L.C.M. as shown below in (a).

(a) 2 = 2 × 1
     4 = 2 × 2   L.C.M. = 20 = 2 × 2 × 5
     5 = 5 × 1

(b) 2 = 2 × 1
     3 = 3 × 1   L.C.M. = 12 = 2 × 2 × 3
     4 = 2 × 2
     6 = 2 × 3   2 and 3 included, no more required

After the children have done several examples they may deduce a method of finding the lowest common multiple as illustrated in (b) above.

To find the L.C.M. of a group of numbers:
(a) write each number in the group as a product of its prime factors,
(b) write down the prime factors of the smallest number,
(c) add to these any factors included in the other numbers which have not been included,
(d) multiply the resulting factors.

Example: Find the L.C.M. of 12 and 15.
12 = 2 × 2 × 3   2 × 2 × 3 × 5 = 60
15 =   3 × 5
L.C.M. of 12 and 15 is 60.
Give examples using this method.

Primary 5 Money

Objectives (a) The children will compare their own currency with Nigeria's naira, Malawi's kwacha, Swaziland's lilangeni, Britain's pounds and America's dollars.

(b) Work problems on profit and loss, simple interest, commission, discount and transactions in the post office.

Knowledge assumed The children will be able to add, subtract, multiply and divide using their own currency. The children know the meaning of percentage and can calculate profit and loss.

Comment This topic is best taught by the formal approach. Information, which cannot be discovered, has to be presented in an interesting way by the teacher. The children would be more interested in the money exchange rates if they know something about the countries concerned. Perhaps it would be possible to teach the children something about these countries in the geography lessons before money exchange is covered in the mathematics lesson.

Teaching aids Map showing countries concerned, examples of money from all countries concerned, tables from paper showing exchange rates on different dates.

Procedure (a) Discuss the money used in the countries concerned. Show the children the actual money used in each country (this can be obtained from a bank). Discuss the pictures and patterns used on the coins and their significance; show the children in which country the money is used by reference to a map.

Give the children examples of exchange rates for the different money. The table overleaf shows the exchange rates for £1 sterling in August 1980 for some countries.

Obtain tables showing the exchange rate for some recent dates (these can be obtained from the bank or from the newspaper). Ensure that the children realize that exchange rates change from day to day. If there is a bank within easy reach of the school perhaps you could persuade someone to come from the bank to explain rates of exchange.

Give the children some practical problems concerning exchange rate and travel; or problems concerning an importer paying for goods from other countries.

Country	Local unit	Exchange for £1
Ghana	Cedi ₵	₵ 4.35
Kenya	Shilling Sh	Sh 19.98
Malawi	Kwacha K	K 1.74
Nigeria	Naira ₦	₦ 1.07
Swaziland	Lilangeni L	L 1.70
U.S.A.	Dollar $	$ 1.56

    (b) Money in social transactions: this topic gives the teacher a real opportunity to show that mathematics is useful in life.

Teaching aids   The teacher should visit the post office, banks and building societies, the tax office and electric supply company to obtain as much literature and information as possible.

    The children should use the information collected to answer questions such as:

1   How much would it cost to make a 6 minute phone call to Nairobi from Mombasa?

2   How much would it cost to talk on the telephone to someone in London if you live in Blantyre?

3   What would a parcel weighing 500g cost to send to any town in your country by post?

4   How much interest would you receive if you invested Sh2000 at 4½% per annum for 3 years?

5   If a farmer bought a goat for Sh240 and sold it for Sh300 what percentage profit will he make?

6   If a single man earned Sh7000 in a year, how much tax would he pay?

    It may be possible to arrange for the children to visit a bank and a post office so that they can see mathematics in action. You may be able to persuade someone to come to your school and explain the services offered by the bank or post office.

Primary 6   *Volume*

Objective   To calculate the volume of a triangular prism and a cylinder.

Knowledge assumed   The children know the meaning of volume as the number of unit cubes necessary to fill a certain space. They can find the volume of cuboids using l × b × h and know how to write cm³. The children have made three D models of cubes and cuboids. They know how to find the area of a rectangle, triangle and circle.

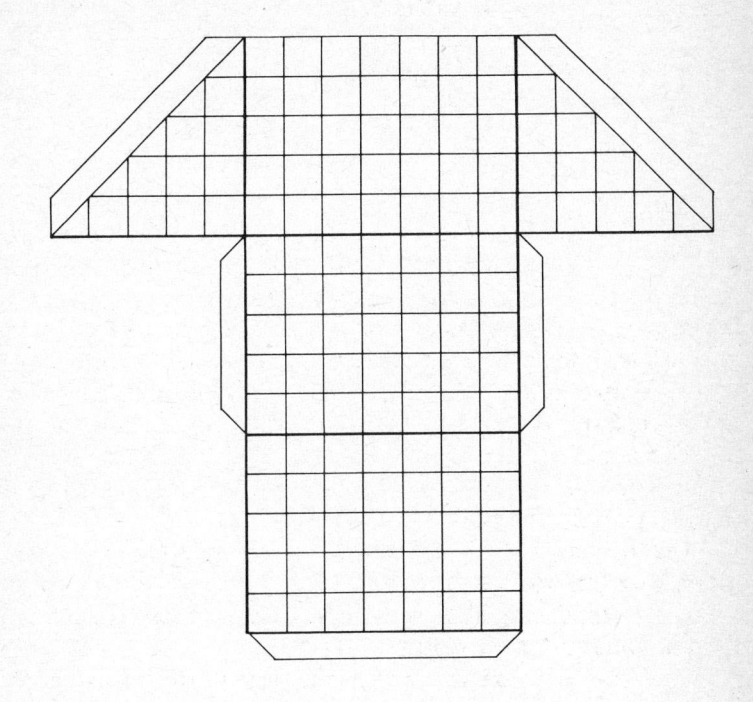

Teaching aids Unit cubes, open cuboid which can be filled with a whole number of unit cubes, a net for a right triangular right angled isosceles prism, 'half' unit cubes, glue and scissors.
Procedure Revise meaning of volume using the open cuboid. Fill the cuboid with centimetre cubes and count the number of cubes. Show again that we can find the volume of a cube by multiplying length by breadth by height. Answer in cm³.

Give each child a copy of a net for a right triangular right angled isosceles prism as shown on page 68.

Ask the children to find the volume of the prism by counting whole and half unit cubes.

Volume = 10 piles of 6 unit cubes + 5 piles of 6 half unit cubes.

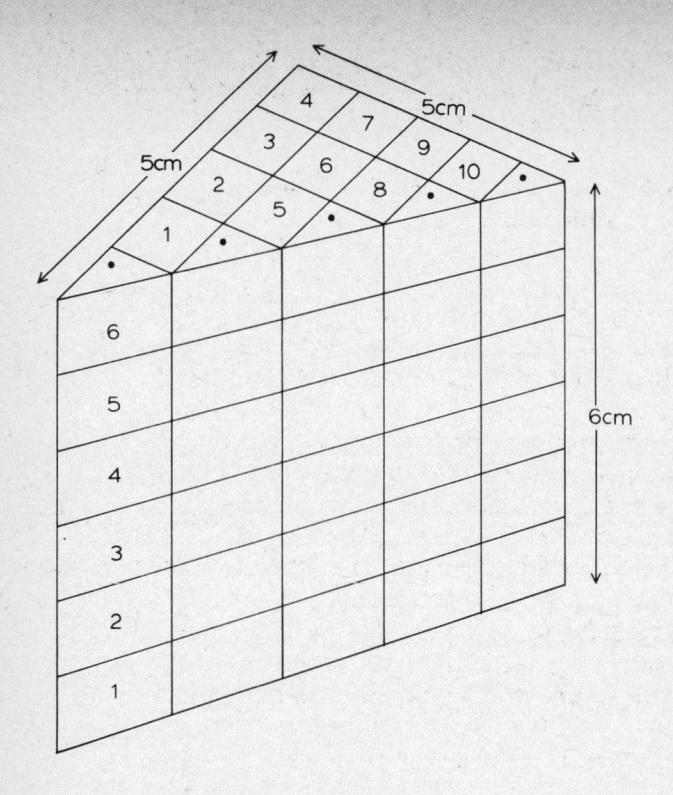

Volume = (10 × 6)+(5 × 6 × ½)
= 60 + 15
= 75 cm³.

Make a model yourself and fill with unit cubes to show that the volume is equal to 75 cm³.

Ask the children if they can find a method for finding the volume of the model. Allow them some time for thought and experimentation.

If no conclusions are reached ask the children if they could find a method of finding the volume of two such prisms. (A cuboid will be formed: volume of 2 prisms = volume of cuboid 5 cm × 5 cm × 6 cm = 150 cm³, ∴ volume of prism = ½ × 5 cm × 5 cm × 6 cm = 75 cm³.)

Ask the children to find the area of the base of the prism. Area of base = ½ × 5 × 5 = 12½ cm³.

Ask the children if they can see the same calculation in our calculation for volume of the prism above.

Ask the children if they could write an explanation of how to find the volume of the prism in terms of the base areas.

Volume of prism = $\underbrace{\frac{1}{2} \times 5 \times 5} \times 6$

= area of base × height.

Return to cuboid

Volume of cuboid = $\underbrace{\text{length} \times \text{breadth}} \times \text{height}$

= area of base × height

The final conclusion to be reached is:

The volume of a right uniform three dimensional object can be found by multiplying area of base × height.

Show the area of the base is equal to the area of cross section. Our conclusion can be written as:

To find the volume of a three dimensional object with uniform cross section we multiply cross sectional area by height.

Give the children some examples to try. Get the children to learn the conclusion off by heart.

When you are sure the children have learnt and understood the conclusion reached, ask them if they can use the conclusion reached to find the volume of a right cylinder.

Volume = X sect. area × height
= $\pi r^2 \times h$
= $\pi r^2 h \; cm^3$

Give some examples for the children to work out.

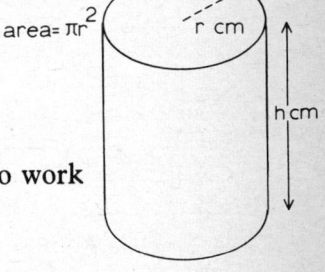

Exercises, Assignments and Projects

1   Comment on the age at which you think the following topics should be taught. Give reasons for your comments.
    (a) Distinguish between horizontal and vertical lines.
    (b) Use Pythogoras' rule to find an unknown length of a right angled triangle.
    (c) Distinguish between odd and even numbers.
    (d) Identify and name cuboids, cylinders and spheres.
    (e) Make meaningful estimates of weights of objects.
2   Choose a topic for each year of the primary school. Explain how you would present the topic.

Chapter Seven

Organizing Children's Work

Classwork

Very often little thought is given to the work children do after they have been taught or have discovered some new process or technique in mathematics. The teacher tells the children to open their text books at page x and to do exercise y. This procedure can of course be all right if the author of the book has followed the same order of teaching as the teacher, and has graded his problems sufficiently finely for the particular class concerned. This, however, is luck rather than good management.

A teacher should spend time deciding what work the class should do and decide when the class should do it. Children enjoy mathematics when they get the answer right. The teacher should make sure the first questions he gives the children are easy enough for the majority of children in the class to get them right. He can give more difficult questions, to stretch the minds of the brighter students, later.

The teacher should make a conscious decision as to when to give the children problems to do. He must be sure that the children have fully understood the concept or technique which has to be taught before he gives them work to do on their own. If the children are given work which they are not capable of doing they will get the answer wrong and become depressed with their ability in mathematics. If the children repeat a wrong process several times they may learn the wrong process and find it very difficult or almost impossible to remember the right process even if it is explained several times afterwards.

A teacher should decide when the class is ready to be given written work by questioning the children. Although he cannot ask each child the same question, he can evaluate the capabilities of each child by asking a question and then pausing for a moment whilst he looks at the eyes of each member of the class. The teacher soon learns to recognize which children do not know the answer. The teacher should make a judgment as to the proportion of the class which does know the answer before naming a particular child to answer.

When he has decided that they will be able to do the problems he has prepared, he should give the children their task and quickly move around the classroom making sure the children are doing the task correctly. If they are not he should stop them from working and spend more time on his explanation. If he finds that most children have missed a particular point he should make note of this so that next year when he is preparing the same lesson he can spend some time thinking about how he could better explain or illustrate the point.

The teacher should decide if all the children in the class should be given the same tasks. For the duller or less able children he may decide to give them an easier exercise. For the brighter children he may decide to give them a longer exercise with more difficult problems at the end. When children have finished their tasks successfully they could be allowed to work on a mathematics project, do some research they have previously been given or answer some questions from a mathematical puzzle book as a reward. Children can become bored with a topic if the teacher gives them more and more similar problems when they already know and have proved for themselves that they know how to carry out the process.

Homework

In many primary schools children in the top forms are given homework to do. Often homework leads to frustration and annoyance on the part of the child and the parents as they watch their child prove to himself *he is no good* and *doesn't know how to do mathematics*.

The problems given for homework should be carefully selected. The children should certainly be able to do the majority of the problems without much difficulty. The reason for giving homework is to make the child rethink what has been learnt in school and practice the new methods or processes. If a child repeats or applies some knowledge recently learnt he will find he remembers more. The teacher should design questions which make the child continually repeat processes already learnt. For example, if we were teaching 'area', when we are sure the children can find the area of rectangles using whole numbers then we could give a problem in area involving the multiplication of fractions or mixed fractions. When we are giving problems on profit and loss we can again include questions which require a knowledge of the process of dealing with fractions, and so on. You will be studying 'memory' in your Psychology course. Read the section on memory and see how you can use the information given to help you to design your teaching in mathematics.

Exercise Books

If you look at mathematics exercise books in primary or secondary school you will find that they are usually covered in numbers and mathematical symbols and usually look most uninteresting. If you turn back ten pages or so and ask the owner of the exercise book what it all means you will find that often he does not know.

If you ask the child if he uses his exercise book when he is revising you will find the answer is no. In most other subjects the child's exercise book is usefully used during revision work. Why should a mathematics exercise book be so different? Do we expect the children to remember everything we have taught them? Do we expect them to remember each process or rule or convention after they have completed a certain number of exercises? If the answer to the last two questions is no, then we must supply notes.

There are many different ways in which the teacher can supply the child with information which will be useful to refresh his memory. Some teachers give notes which the children copy down, others give out duplicated notes, others allow the children to write their own notes (the notes being corrected by the teacher afterwards). Some teachers give notes which are copied down in a special mathematics note book, others prefer to give notes before each exercise so that the notes are followed by worked examples which the child can study later.

The method used will depend on the age of the children, their capabilities and whether they have been trained in note taking. In the exercises at the end of this chapter you will be asked to discuss what methods you think are most appropriate at different age levels.

Note Books

Let us discuss what type of note taking would be useful and how it should be organized.

The opinion of many teachers who use mathematics note books is that a special exercise book should be kept for notes. The child carries his note book from one year to the next and has a permanent record or summary of all his previous work in mathematics.

The note book can be made to look attractive by using different coloured paper which is stuck into the exercise book when appropriate. For example, when finding area of a triangle $= \frac{1}{2}bh$, coloured paper can be used for the diagrams.

One way of organizing the note book is as follows:

The first few pages are kept to fill in a contents list. Half the book is reserved for notes. The next quarter of the book is reserved for 'things I must learn by heart'. The last quarter of the book is used for a vocabulary and symbols list. As a new word or symbol is met it is added to the list together with a suitably worded definition. The definition found in a dictionary is often too complicated for primary children to understand. The teacher should write definitions suitable for the age range he is teaching. To show how the note book could look we have shown primary mathematics topics below with the appropriate notes.

Topic

Practical and descriptive geometry Primary 6
Objective
>The children will be able to
>(a) identify parallel and perpendicular lines,
>(b) state some properties of plane 4 sided shapes.

Knowledge assumed
>The children will be able to
>(a) identify squares, rectangles and triangles,
>(b) state the properties of squares and rectangles,
>(c) draw squares and rectangles.

Teaching aids

Pieces of string, rubber bands, drawing pins, rulers, set squares, nail board, cutouts of different sized and shaped parallelograms, squares, rectangles, rhombi, duplicated shapes preferably on coloured paper, for children to cut out and use in their notes, glue, pencils, pens, and so on.

Procedure

As this chapter is concerned with the notes to be taken we are not going into detail on procedure. It will take several periods to cover the objectives stated above. The children will have to be shown the meaning of parallel and perpendicular lines and be given the names of the new shapes, i.e. parallelogram, rhombus, kite and also the meaning of a diagonal. Using the materials explained above in *'Teaching aids'* the children can find the properties of the different shapes themselves.

Vocabulary

This topic has been chosen to illustrate the point that vocabulary should be considered because it contains a number of new words. When we start to think of all the new words the children meet in this topic it is not surprising that they have difficulty remembering what they have 'learned'. In all topics there are new words and the teacher should make sure the children know the meaning of the words.

In this topic the following new words or phrases will be met by the children:

(i) plane surface and figure, (ii) opposite corner or angle,
(iii) parallel lines, (iv) parallelogram,
(v) diagonal, (vi) rhombus,
(vii) kite, (viii) intersect, and
(ix) bisect.

These phrases or words might be explained in our vocabulary list as shown below.

Plane surface
The chalk board, the top of the teacher's desk, a window pane all have flat surfaces. In mathematics we say these are plane surfaces.

Plane figure
If a closed figure is drawn on a plane surface we say it is a plane figure.

Opposite corner or angles

Opposite means facing front to front or back to back. Here are some examples of

(a) opposite sides

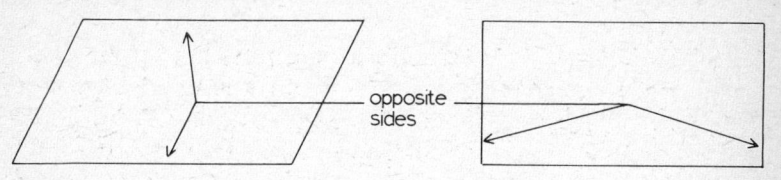

(b) opposite angles

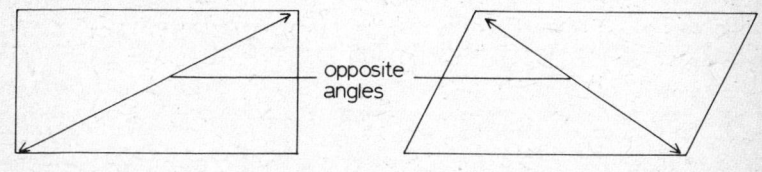

Parallel lines

We say two straight lines are parallel when they stay the same distance apart no matter how far they are extended. The opposite sides of a rectangle are parallel to each other. No matter how far we extend them they will not meet.

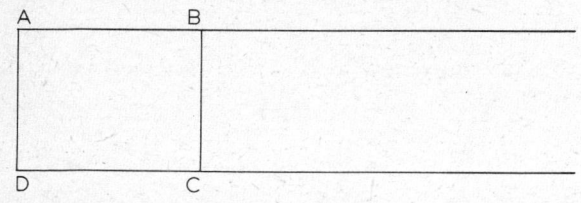

AD is also parallel to BC.

Parallelogram

A parallelogram is a four sided plane figure whose opposite sides are parallel. In the figure AB is parallel to DC and AD is parallel to BC.

A square and a rectangle can be considered as special cases of a parallelogram.

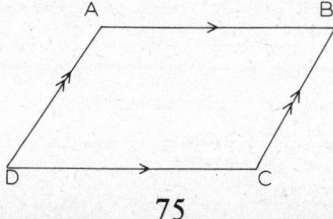

Diagonal

A diagonal is a straight line joining the opposite corners of any plane four sided figure. Here are some examples of diagonals.

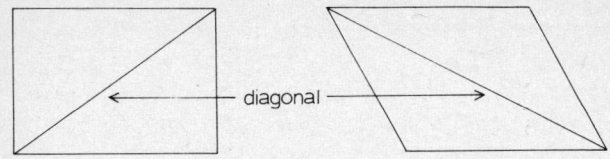

Rhombus

A rhombus is a parallelogram in which all four sides are equal.

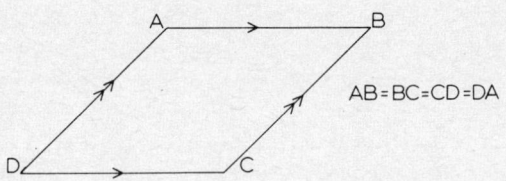

AB = BC = CD = DA

Kite

A kite is a four sided plane figure with two pairs of sides next to each other (adjacent) equal in length.

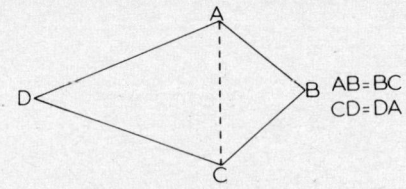

AB = BC
CD = DA

Intersect

When two lines cross each other they are said to intersect; the point at which they cross is called the point of intersection.

Bisect

To cut or divide into two parts.

When we write out the meaning of the new words the children have met we appreciate that the children have a lot to learn. Most mathematics teachers, however, expect the children to know the words and their meanings with little or no teaching. If the same words were met in an English comprehension passage the teacher would spend a considerable time teaching the children the new words.

Notes

Note taking, as mentioned previously, can be done in many different ways. The children could be asked to write their own notes; the notes would be corrected by the teacher.

Partial notes could be duplicated, gaps being left for the children to fill in.

Questions could be asked which the children have to answer with a 'yes' or a 'no', a tick or cross, or with a short phrase or sentence.

Some of these techniques are illustrated below.

Plane shapes and their properties
A square

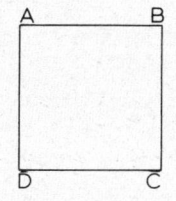

A square has four ———. The edges are ——— in length. The corners are ———. If a straight line is drawn joining opposite corners the lines are called ———. The diagonals of a square are ——— in length.

A rectangle

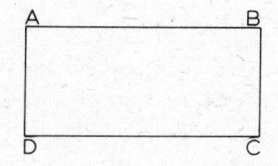

A rectangle has ——— straight ———. The opposite sides of a ——— are ——— in length. The corners are ———. The ——— of a rectangle are ——— in length.

Parallel lines

The opposite edges of a square or a rectangle are ———. If we produce any pair of ——— edges of a square or rectangle the lines will ——— meet. The lines always stay the same ——— apart. The lines are ———.

A parallelogram

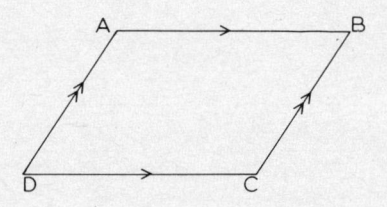

The opposite ——— of a ——— are ——— in length. The opposite edges of a parallelogram are ———. The diagonals of a parallelogram ——— each other. The arrows on the diagram show which lines are ———.

A rhombus

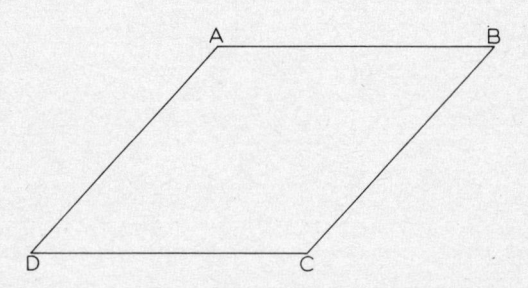

The four edges of a rhombus are ——— in length. The opposite edges of a ——— are also ———. The marks on the lines **AB**, **BC** etc. show that ——— = ——— = ——— = ———. The diagonals of a rhombus are ——— in length. The diagonals of a rhombus ——— each other. The diagonals meet forming a ——— ———; and so on for a kite and trapezium.

A summary of the findings of the children's experiments could be written in table as shown below:

Question	square	rect-angle	paral-lelogram	rhom-bus	trap-ezium	kite
Are opposite sides equal?						
Are opposite sides parallel?						
Are the diagonals equal in length?						
Do the diagonals cut each other in two equal parts?						
Does the figure have square corners?						
Are opposite corners of equal size?						
Do the diagonals bisect at right angles?						
Are all the sides the same length?						

Perhaps it is easier to produce notes for the descriptive type of mathematics as shown above. We show below two examples of the types of notes for descriptive topics in mathematics which will be useful to children if they have forgotten the topic.

Example I
Factors

One number can be replaced by two numbers which when multiplied together give the first number.

Here are some examples: 12 = 3 × 4
6 = 2 × 3
7 = 7 × 1

3 and 4 are called factors of 12.

As 7 can only be replaced by 7 and × 1 we call it a prime factor.

12 has many factors; it can be divided by 1, 2, 3, 4, 6 and 12, without leaving a remainder.

Every number has a factor of 1 and itself so we tend to be lazy and leave these two factors out.

We say the factors of 12 are 2, 3, 4 and 6.

The factors of 21 are 3 and 7.

Lowest common multiple

The lowest common multiple is the smallest number into which a given group of numbers can be divided, in turn, without leaving a remainder.

If each number in the group must be divided into the L.C.M. without leaving a remainder, the L.C.M. must be equal to or greater than the largest number in the group.

Example

Find the L.C.M. of 6 and 14.

The multiples of 6 are 6,12,18,24,30,36,**42**,48,54,60,66,72, 78,**84**, and so on.

The multiples of 14 are   14,   28,   **42**,   56,   70, **84**, and so on. The lowest common multiple is 42.

We can find the L.C.M. using the method below.

1. Write down the numbers of the group in terms of their prime factors: 6 = 2 × 3, 14 = 2 × 7.
2. Write down the prime factors of the smallest number: 2 × 3.
3. Add to this any factor from the other number which has not already been written: 2 × 3 × 7
4. Multiply these factors: 2 × 3 × 7 = 42

Here is another example.

Find the L.C.M. of 12 and 15.

12 = 2 × 2 × 3   15 = 3 × 5
L.C.M. = 2 × 2 × 3 × 5 = 60.

Example II

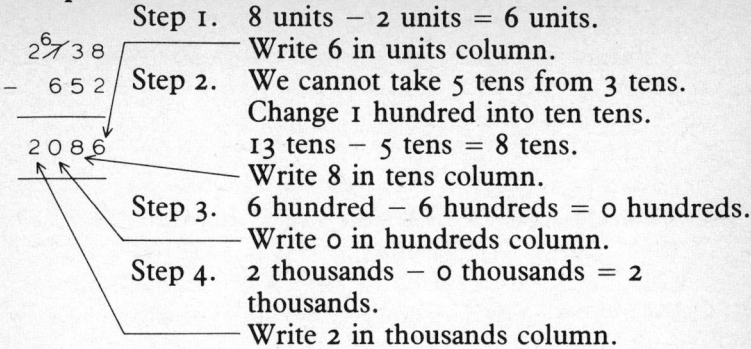

$$\begin{array}{r} 2\overset{6}{\cancel{7}}3\,8 \\ -6\,5\,2 \\ \hline 2\,0\,8\,6 \end{array}$$

Step 1. 8 units − 2 units = 6 units.
Write 6 in units column.

Step 2. We cannot take 5 tens from 3 tens. Change 1 hundred into ten tens.
13 tens − 5 tens = 8 tens.
Write 8 in tens column.

Step 3. 6 hundred − 6 hundreds = 0 hundreds.
Write 0 in hundreds column.

Step 4. 2 thousands − 0 thousands = 2 thousands.
Write 2 in thousands column.

Notes for Revision

If we repeat or revise a topic we remember so much more. A good study habit to train the children in is to revise their knowledge frequently. We have already said we meet a topic in class, and the knowledge gained is applied in homework tasks. Further repeats are built into our teaching, for example giving length of $3\frac{1}{2}$ cm and breadth of $2\frac{1}{4}$ cm when doing problems on area. Besides these it is a good idea to have periodic revision sessions. In these sessions the class discusses what they have learnt in, say, the last month and they produce a summary of what they have learnt. These summaries are kept as they will be useful to the children when they are revising for end of term exams.

Exercises, Assignments and Projects

1. For a primary mathematics topic of your own choice design a series of question suitable for (a) the less able members of a class, (b) the average group in the class, and (c) the bright members of a class. Explain why you think the particular questions are suitable for each group.
2. Find out as much as you can about how people remember things. Discuss how the study can help you design a better course in mathematics for primary children.
3. Study the exercises given for the same topic in mathematics in several text books. Decide which exercise is the best and say why.

4   The lists below show some of the vocabulary met by children in different primary classes. Show how you would define the meaning of each word. Remember children in primary 1 and 2 can read only a few words. Consult a primary reading scheme to ensure you do not use words in your definitions that they have not already met.

Primary 1	*Primary 2*	*Primary 3*
compare	fraction	numerator
fewer than	unequal	factor
more than	odd number	remainder
comes before	combination	multiples
equal	carrying	perimeter
rectangle	multiplication	area
heavier than	largest	estimate
shorter than	minute	litre

Primary 4	*Primary 5*	*Primary 6*
decimal fraction	million	equation
square of a number	percentage	rates
digit	ratio	square root
square	H.C.F.	trapezium
triangle	equivalents	perpendicular
properties	simple interest	tally
circle	transaction	a degree (angles)
symmetrical	pi	mode

5   Show the type of notes you think the children should take on a primary mathematics topic of your own choice.
6   Write a set of revision notes which you think would be suitable for:
   (a) a primary 3 child on multiplication,
   (b) a primary 4 child on fractions,
   (c) a primary 5 child on ratio and percentage,
   (d) a primary 6 child on finding the volume of a triangular prism and a cylinder.
7   Visit a few local primary schools; study the children's exercise (and note) books.
8   Discuss which method of note taking you think most appropriate for each primary class.

Chapter Eight

Evaluation

In this chapter we are concerned with the general principles of evaluating mathematics learnt by the children in the primary school. Testing and measurement is a wide topic and many texts have been written on the subject. The questions we want to answer in this chapter are the following. Can we make tests to find out what the children are having difficulty with? Can we make tests to help us group children into sets? Can we make tests which will give us reliable information on the achievements of a child so that our reports to parents are meaningful? Can we check that our tests are reliable and valid? Can we ensure that our tests help the students to learn rather than help to destroy their confidence? Are tests available which we can use so that we can compare the ability of our children with children of similar age?

Can we make tests to find out what the children are having difficulty with?

The main task of a teacher is to communicate ideas to the children. He must continually assess how successful he has been and try and fill in the gaps he has found. One of the difficulties in mathematics is that often the study of a new topic depends on the mastery of one or more topics which have been learnt before. A small break or hole in the chain may mean a child is doomed to failure in his further study of mathematics.

When we test a child's ability in mathematics we should remember we are also testing our ability as teachers to communicate our ideas. If the majority of the children in the class cannot do a particular problem it probably means we have not communicated a process or concept sufficiently well.

If the children cannot do a particular problem it does not mean that they haven't learnt anything. It might mean that all the children have forgotten one step in the process. It might mean that each child has made a different slip and hence arrived at the wrong answer. A car can be basically sound and yet it will not work if the petrol supply is broken or the spark does not reach the plugs. If a car does not work a mechanic will carry out certain general tests to find the source of the trouble. He will then test the electrical system, for example, in more detail if he suspects that the difficulty is there. He diagnoses the fault and then tries to correct it.

When we find children are getting the wrong answer to a particular problem we may be able to find the cause by looking more carefully at the 'working'. A common error of teachers when marking mathematics is that they think they should only be concerned with seeing if the answer is right or wrong. (We will discuss marking in more detail later.) What they should really be concerned with is why the child has got the wrong answer if it is wrong.

Let us consider a simple addition sum.

```
  1 6 0 3     Here are some answers obtained from a group
+   5 9 8     of children when asked to do this sum:
  -------
  2 2 0 1     221, 2211, 1191, 1005, and 1001.
  -------
```

See if you can work out the error made by each child before you read on.

Answer 221. The child has added 8 and 3 correctly, he has carried 1 ten and added it to 9 tens giving 10 tens. He has carried 1 hundred but has not put a zero in the tens column. He may have just forgotten to put the zero down or he may have thought, as many children do, that nought means nothing so we don't need to write it.

Answer 2211. Again, nearly right; $8 + 3 = 11$ – one down, carry 1; $1 + 9 + 0 = 11$. The child's reasoning is: 'Well, $1 + 9 = 10$, $10 + 0 = 11$; there is something written there (0) and the least we can count it as is 1 zero'. Another common error.

Answer 1191. This child has forgotten to carry 1 ten and 1 hundred.

```
  1 1 9 1
+ 1 0 1 0
  -------
  2 2 0 1
  -------
```

Answer 1005. This child has subtracted instead of adding.

Answer 1001. This child has added correctly in the units and tens column, subtracted in the hundreds column, and we cannot tell whether he has added or subtracted in the thousands column.

In the above cases we have been lucky – we have diagnosed the problems without further testing, but each case has been a puzzle. Sometimes we cannot find a solution. We have seen, however, that by taking time over marking we can often spot the difficulty. We can then either write a comment on the exercise book or explain the error to the child. If we cannot spot the error we should make a note to ask the child to explain how he worked out the sum.

If we still cannot spot the error we have to produce a diagnostic test which will tell us where the gap in knowledge lies.

In order to find the error we have to produce a test which tests each difficulty separately.

The difficulties in the sum under discussion are difficulties with carrying, difficulties with zero in the addition, difficulties with zero in the answer and perhaps difficulties with the number bonds.

Our diagnostic test would be:

Testing:

(a) 3 + 8 =   number bond
    6 + 5 =   number bond

(b) 1 0   zero in addition; note no other
  +1 4   difficulty in carrying
  ———

(c) 1 6   zero in first column of answer; note
  +3 4   simple number bonds
  ———

(d) 1 1 5 2   zero in 2nd column of answer
    1 5 4
  ————

(e) 1 4   carrying
  +2 8
  ———

To produce a diagnostic test we analyse a topic or problem, find all the steps involved in the problem and test each step separately.

Can we make tests to group children into sets?

If we are teaching in a school where there are two or three streams we may wish to divide the children into set A and B for mathematics. If there is a large difference between the children in a single stream class we may wish to divide the children into two or three groups to be dealt with separately. What kind of test should we produce?

If we wish to divide the class or group of children into two sets we should produce a test in which approximately a third of the questions are easy and the rest are difficult. We should always include some easy questions in a test, preferably at the beginning. We should do this for two reasons:

(a) Most students start an examination in an agitated state; if they find they can deal with the first few questions with no trouble they settled down and achieve of their best; (b) no student likes to obtain zero for a test; if they do they will feel like putting no effort into the subject in the future.

If we design a test in which one third of the test items are easy and the rest are difficult we will obtain a distribution of marks as shown in the graph below. To draw the graph we have found the number of children obtaining marks between 1 and 10; 11 and 20; 21 and 30, and so on. This type of graph is called a frequency distribution.

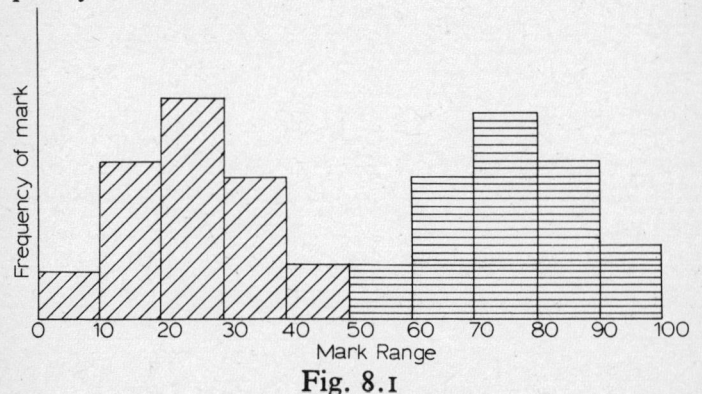

Fig. 8.1

From the graph it can be seen that there is a group of students who should definitely be in the lower group (shaded ▨), and a group of students who should be in the upper group (shaded ▤). We will have to look at the students who have obtained marks of between 40 and 50 in more detail before we can decide if they are to be in the top or lower set.

How do we know if a question is difficult or not?

In order to know which type of questions are easy or difficult for a particular age range we have to learn by experience.

When you mark questions which you give to the children, you should find out what percentage of the children in your class have obtained the correct solution. This does not take much time. As you are marking you have a sheet of paper next to you with the number of questions down the margin. Every time a child obtains the correct answer we put a tick next to the appropriate question number. You would obtain a chart similar to the one shown below.

1	✓✓✓✓✓✓✓✓✓✓✓✓✓✓✓✓✓✓✓✓	20
2	✓✓✓✓✓✓✓✓✓✓✓✓✓✓✓✓	16
3	✓✓✓✓✓✓✓✓✓✓✓✓✓✓✓✓✓✓✓✓✓✓✓✓	24
4	✓✓✓✓✓✓✓✓✓✓✓✓	12
5	✓✓✓✓✓✓✓✓✓	9

If there were 36 children taking the test $\frac{20}{36} \times 100\%$ of the children obtained the correct answer for number 1, i.e. approximately 55% of the children obtained the correct answer. We say the facility level of the question (or item) is 55% or the difficulty level is 45%.

Similarly it can be calculated that the facility and difficulty levels of the five items illustrated are:

Question	Facility level	Difficulty level
1	55	45
2	44	56
3	66.6	33.3
4	33.3	66.6
5	25	75

If we find the difficulty levels for each question we give the children in a test or class work and record it, we will soon become familiar with the difficulty level of certain types of questions. If we keep the difficulty levels of tests over a few

87

Fig. 8.2

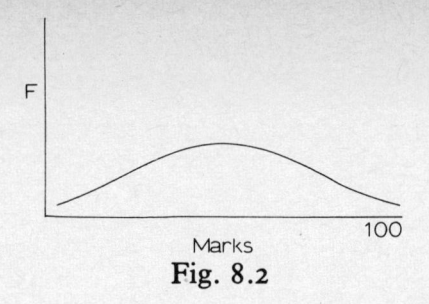

years we will be able to use items again knowing the difficulty levels before we set the examination. If we wish to design a test to spread the children over the whole marking scale as shown in Fig. 8.2, we would pick items which have a difficulty level of between 40% and 60%. A test like this would be ideal as an end of term test as we are attempting to spread the children over a wide range of marks so that we can distinguish between them. Remember to include some items with a difficulty level of below 10% to encourage the weaker child.

Does the difficulty level tell us anything else?

When teachers mark homework and classwork, they are mostly concerned with finding a total mark or percentage for each child. This is useful; it tells us if the child is maintaining his standard of work. It does not, however, give the teacher much indication of what the children in the class, as a whole, have learnt. If, however, we find the difficulty level of each item in a test we know what topics are difficult or have been badly taught.

If the difficulty level of a question is say 10% we can conclude that the topic has been well learnt. If the difficulty level is 80% there is no doubt that the topic needs reteaching. The difficulty levels give us, as teachers, an indication of the success of our teaching and show us what our next step should be.

Can we construct a test to find the children requiring remedial treatment?

If we design a test in which the difficulty level of most items is approximately 30% we will obtain a frequency distribution as shown in Fig. 8.3. Most of the children will obtain high marks.

Fig. 8.3

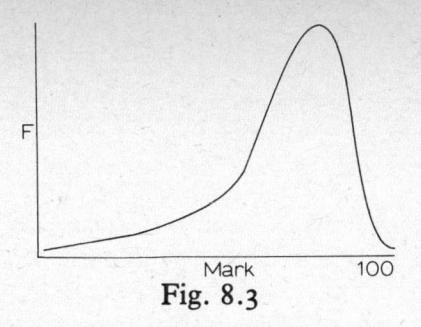

The poorer children will be spread over a large range of marks. We can distinguish between the weak and very weak children.

Can we construct a test to find the very bright child?

If we construct a test in which the majority of items have a difficulty level of 70% and above we will obtain a frequency distribution as shown in Fig. 8.4. Most of the children will obtain low marks. The brighter children will be spread over a large range of marks. We will be able to distinguish between the bright and the very bright child.

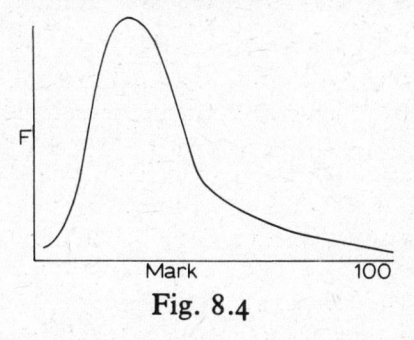

Fig. 8.4

If you, as a teacher, use a test to find the bright children, it is advisable not to publish the marks to the children. Publishing the marks achieves no positive purpose; it will only depress the children.

Can we make tests which will give us reliable information on the achievements of children so that our reports to parents are meaningful?

When we are designing a test, the result of which will be a

report to parents, our objective is to produce a single mark which will explain a child's achievement in mathematics throughout the year. Quite a task and certainly a task which should be taken seriously.

How can we attempt to design a test which will achieve this aim? As we become more experienced with testing and become more aware of the difficulty level of items we write for a particular class, our task will become easier.

We are aiming at a test which will discriminate between the children in the class. We wish to produce a distribution of scores over a large range. We wish to produce a distribution similar to the one shown in figure 8.2. To achieve this we can select items which have a difficulty level of between 40% and 60%.

Besides this we must sample the year's syllabus as far as possible; items should be chosen so that the majority of topics covered during the year are tested. If this is not the case the children who have revised the topics we test will have an unfair advantage. Children soon learn if a teacher does not cover the work done in his testing and consequently spot favourite topics of the teacher and just revise these.

Can we check that our tests are reliable and valid?
Reliable

When we say a test is reliable we mean that the test will place a given group of students in the same order if the test is given to the same students on two separate occasions. If the test claims to place children in order of merit it should be able to do so consistently, i.e. the test should be reliable.

Here are two ways in which you can test whether your test is reliable.

Method I: Test retest

Give the test to the children on two different occasions. Plot a graph of marks obtained by each child on first testing against marks obtained on the repeated test.

If you obtain a graph similar to the one shown in figure 8.5 you can say your test is reliable.

If you find that the points are distributed over a circle as shown in figure 8.6 then the test is unreliable. If the points are distributed as in 8.6 it means that some children who have

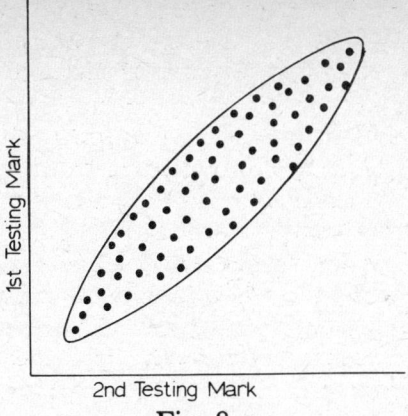

Fig. 8.5

obtained a high mark when first tested obtained a low mark when tested on the second occasion, and vice versa. The test is therefore unreliable.

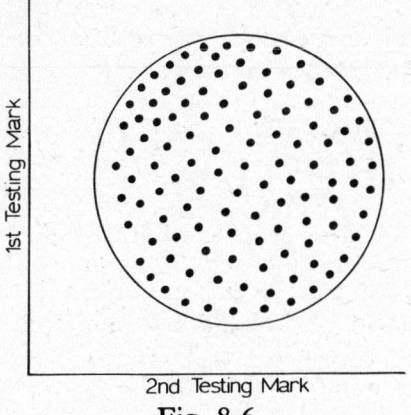

Fig. 8.6

Method II: One testing
When we give a test we are assuming that each question in the test is testing the child's ability in mathematics. If we gave the children half the questions in our test these questions should place the children in the same order as the total test or the other half of the test.

To 'test' the reliability of our test we find the scores obtained by each child on the odd numbered questions and the even numbered questions. We then plot these scores on a graph as shown in figure 8.7. Again if we obtain a scatter of points in the shape of a narrow ellipse we can say the test is reliable.

Score on odd numbered questions

Score on even numbered questions

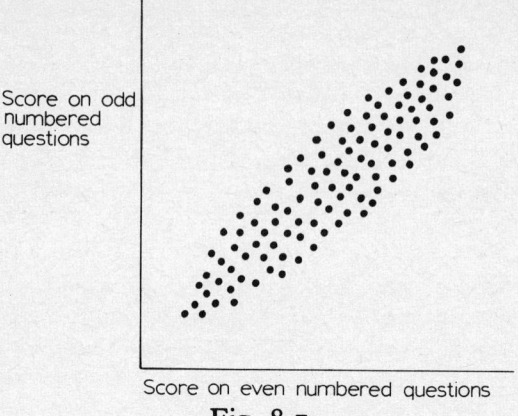

Fig. 8.7

These diagrams, figures 8.5 to 8.7, we have drawn are called scatter diagrams. They show the relationship between first testing and second testing. If the points all lie on a straight line we would say there was a simple relation between the two variables. The more scattered they become the further away we get from being able to draw a useful conclusion.

There is a mathematical process to obtain a single number to explain these graphs. (If you wish to know how to calculate this number consult an Educational Measurement book.)

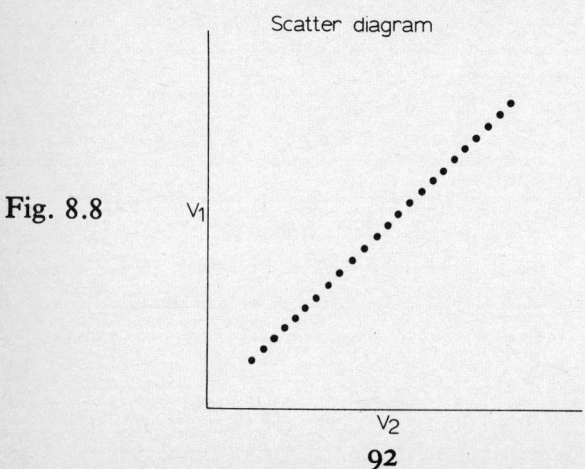

Scatter diagram

Fig. 8.8

V_1

V_2

If our scatter diagram becomes a straight line we obtain a number 1.

If our scatter diagram looks like figure 8.5 we obtain a number of about 0.86.

If our scatter diagram looks like figure 8.6 we will obtain a number near 0. The numbers obtained are called correlation coefficients. If the number or correlation coefficient is towards 1 we can say with reasonable confidence that, for example, our test is reliable. You will meet the word correlation coefficient in your Psychology books.

Valid

When we say a test is valid we mean it tests what it is supposed to test.

You might think this a peculiar thing to say. Of course a 'test' tests what it is supposed to test! A mathematics 'test' tests mathematics, an English 'test' tests English and so on. But is this always the case?

We could write a Physics test which required such a knowledge of mathematics that it is a test in mathematics.

We could write a mathematics test using difficult words or difficult sentence constructions: the test becomes a test in English rather than mathematics.

When we have finished writing our test we should always look at it critically and ask ourselves, 'is it testing mathematics? Is the English level sufficiently low? Are there any sentences which are long and complicated and difficult to understand? Are there any ambiguities?' You could ask another teacher to

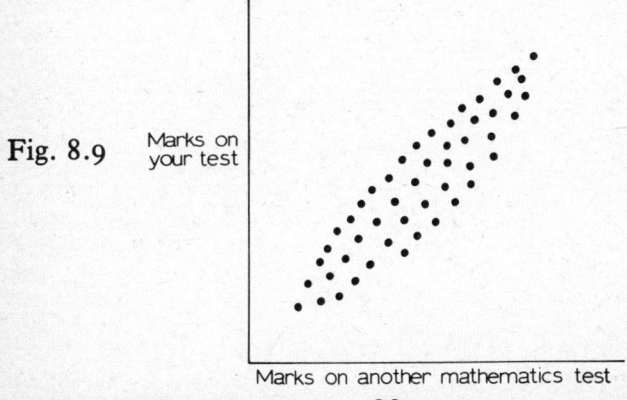

Fig. 8.9

'do' your test. Ask him to answer the three questions above. If you follow this process you will be reasonably confident that your test is valid. We say the test has face validity.

One method of testing the validity of a test is to give the same group of students your test and another test on mathematics. Again we draw a scatter diagram. If the two tests are testing the same thing they should put the children in the same order. We should obtain a scatter diagram as shown in figure 8.9 if our test is valid. Note we are assuming that the test we are comparing our test with is a valid mathematics test. If we obtain a graph in which the points are contained in a 'narrow' ellipse we would say the test has concurrent validity.

Did our test achieve its purpose?

When we have marked our test we should always draw a frequency distribution. A study of the distribution curve will tell us if we chose the right questions to obtain the distribution we required.

Reporting to parents

Let us consider some possible distributions we might obtain from our testing.

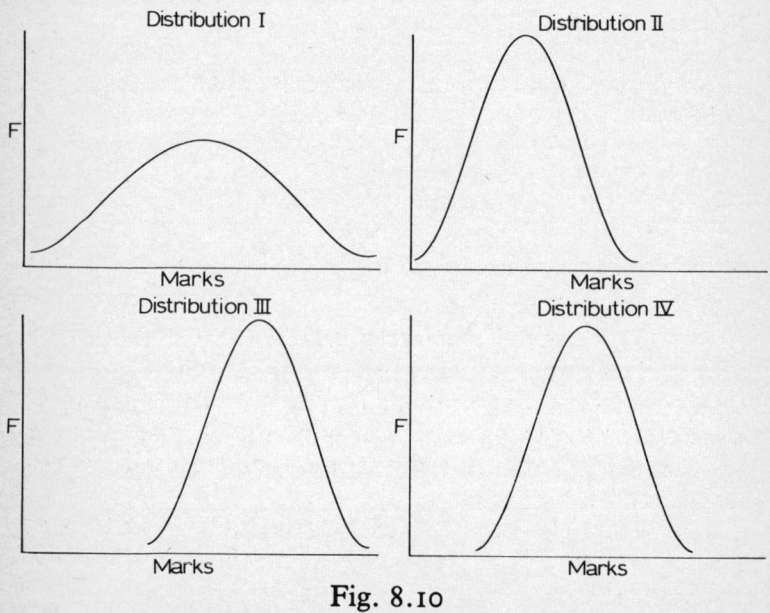

Fig. 8.10

If we obtain a distribution as in I we have produced a good test.

If we obtain a distribution as in II our test was too difficult.

If we obtain a distribution as in III our test was too easy.

If we obtain a distribution as in IV nearly all children have obtained a mark of about 50. Our test has not shown any difference between the majority of candidates. The test has not discriminated between them. It has not achieved its purpose.

If we are asked to report scores to parents a score of 50% will mean different things depending on the distribution it has come from. If a child obtains 50% in the test which has produced the distribution I the child is average. If he obtained 50% in the test which produced distribution II he is very good – probably 2nd or 3rd in the class. If he obtained 50% in the test which produced distribution III he would be bottom of the class. The marks obtained in the test which have produced distribution IV are of little or no use as a change of 3 or 4 marks either way can make a difference of being 10th in the class or 30th.

From the above discussion we can see that reporting a score on its own will not give the parents any information at all. To give the mark more meaning we can report the mark, the position in class in that subject, and pass some remark on the child's progress during the term.

Some schools report scores so that they have a definite meaning according to a key given at the bottom of the report for example.

	18	32	43	55	62	75	
0	10	20 30	40	50	60	70	80
Very poor		Poor	Below average	Average	Good	Very good	Excellent

If this is the case the marks obtained on this test which produced distribution I can easily be reported on.

If we convert the marks obtained in the test which produced distribution II, using this key, most students will receive a poor report; similarly for distribution III most students will receive excellent reports.

If we have designed a test which was too difficult we have to change our marks before reporting to parents. Consider the distribution II.

The children in area 1 are very poor, in area 2 are poor, in area 3 are below average, in area 4 are average, and so on.

A score of 12 on our test is a score of 18 on the key shown above. A score of 18 on our test is equivalent to a score of 32 on the key shown above, and so on.

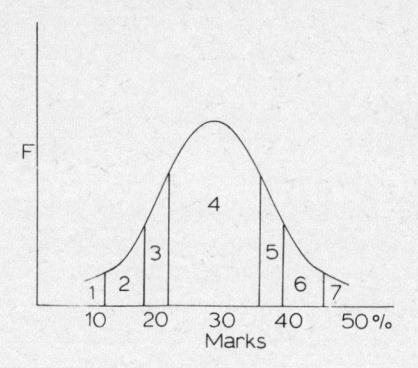

Fig. 8.11

If it is necessary to report scores which are interpreted according to a key and we have given a test which is too difficult we can change the scores by arguing equivalent points on our distribution and adjusting marks within the bands or grades by simple proportion.

Can we ensure that our tests help students to learn rather than help to destroy their confidence?

As we have said previously a test can be oral questions, work done in class or a formal test or examination. The way a teacher reacts to the children's response to any of these forms of testing can affect the child's attitude to the subject.

Many teachers have the attitude that a response to a mathematics problem is either right or wrong. In consequence the child gets no recognition of the effort he has made to obtain the correct answer: he gets low marks and is depressed. In every other subject marks are given for effort. Why should the marking of mathematics be so different?

Let us consider some examples.

Example I

```
   2 4
   3 3 8
  +9 0 8
  ───────
  1 2 7 0
  ───────
   2
```

If a child has written 0 in the first column but forgotten to add the 2 to the second column he will obtain an answer of 1250. Surely he has shown that he has some understanding of the process of addition and deserves at least half marks.

Example II

Multiply 2.3 by 2.8 using the method of multiplying by parts.

Let us suppose the child responds as follows:

$$\begin{aligned}
2.3 \times 2.8 &= 2.3 \, (2 \, + \, 0.8) \\
&= (2.3 \times 2) + (2.3 \times 0.8) \\
&= (2 \times 2) + (2 \times 0.3) + (2 \times 0.8) \\
&\quad + (0.3 \times 0.8) \\
&= 4 \, + \, 0.6 \, + \, 1.6 \, + \, 2.4 \\
&= 8.7
\end{aligned}$$

He has made an error in multiplying 0.3×0.8 and an error in his final addition.

He has, however, shown that he understands the method of multiplying by parts and deserves to be rewarded for this.

Our marking scheme for this question should be as follows:

	Marks
$2.3 \times 2.8 = 2.3 \, (2 + 0.8)$	1
$= (2.3 \times 2) + (2.3 \times 0.8)$	1
$= (2 \times 2) + (2 \times 0.3) + (2 \times 0.8)$	
$\quad + (0.3 \times 0.8)$	2
$= 4 \, + \, 0.6 \, + \, 1.6 \, + \, 0.24$	1
$= 6.44$	1

giving one mark for each major step in the calculation.

We may decide that if a child makes a slip between line 3 and line 4 but adds his numbers on line 4 correctly then he gets the mark for the last line.

A child could therefore score 5 marks out of 6 and yet have the answer wrong. He has been rewarded for his efforts and feels it is worthwhile trying.

Are tests available which we can use so that we can compare the ability of our children with children of similar ages?

Tests which have been given to a large number of children and have been tested for reliability and validity have been produced in other countries and are for sale. As the tests have been given to a large number of children they have found the average score for children of different ages, for example 10.5 year olds, on the test. If a child obtains this score he is said to have a 'mathematical' age of 10.5 years. If his present age is 11 years old then he is not up to standard. If his present age is 9 years old then he is excellent. This type of test is called a standardized test. Unfortunately standardized tests have not as yet been produced for Nigeria.

If you use standardized tests from other countries you should read them carefully and decide if all the questions can be understood by your children. Results from such a test would give you some idea of how your children compare with children of a similar age. You should expect your children to get slightly lower marks if there are questions or diagrams in the test which they cannot understand readily.

Addresses of firms from which you can buy standardized tests are given at the end of this book.

Exercises, Projects and Assignments

1. Choose a primary mathematics topic. Design a test suitable to find the difficulties children are having with learning the topic.
2. Write a test for a particular age range. Try it out in a local primary school. Find the difficulty levels for each question. Draw the distribution curve and comment on it.
3. Produce a marking scheme for the test produced in 2. Explain why you decided to give marks to particular sections of the answer.
4. Find out how different primary schools in your area report to parents on the progress of their children.
5. Obtain an example of a standardized test in mathematics. Comment on its suitability for use locally.

Chapter Nine

Records and Classroom Organization

Records
If we asked teachers why they kept records they would say they kept them so that at the end of term they can add up the marks and hence will be able to comment on the progress of each child during the term.

This is a very good reason for keeping records but it is not the only reason.

We keep records so that we can get to know as much as we can about a particular child, so that we can help him as an individual and help him enjoy mathematics.

We start our records with a list of names and a class plan showing where each child sits. If we write the names of the children on the left hand side of our mark book, or squared paper exercise book, as shown in figure 9.1, we can cut strips off the next 4 or so pages so that we can use the same name list for each page.

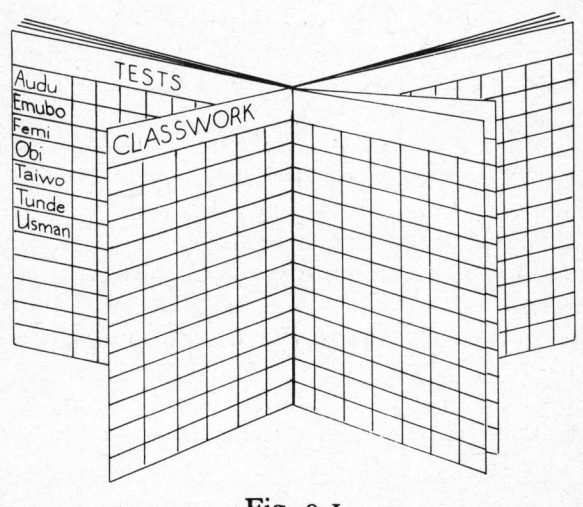

Fig. 9.1

What type of records do we keep on all these pages? We could keep one page for the results of tests. If we keep a copy of each test we give and number them we will be able to see to which tests the scores apply if we number the columns in our mark book accordingly.

We could keep the second page for classwork marks. Classwork marks tend to be rather higher than test scores as the children are doing the problems immediately after they have been taught a topic. The classwork marks do not reflect the child's ability to recall information after some passage of time.

The third and fourth pages could be kept for keeping results of diagnostic tests. Again we should keep a copy of each diagnostic test we give the children. Our records will be more useful to us if we show the mark for each question in the test. We could label each column showing the particular difficulty which is being tested by the item, for example:

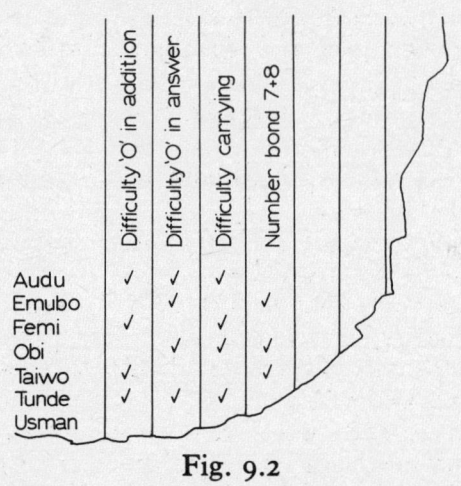

	Difficulty 'O' in addition	Difficulty 'O' in answer	Difficulty carrying	Number bond 7+8
Audu	✓	✓	✓	
Emubo		✓		✓
Femi	✓		✓	✓
Obi		✓	✓	✓
Taiwo	✓.			✓
Tunde	✓	✓	✓	
Usman				

Fig. 9.2

These records can now be referred to in the future so that we can help each child with his particular difficulty. When, for example, Femi has learnt how to deal with 'O' in an answer we can 'tick' the appropriate space in our records with a different coloured pen. We will then know Femi originally had difficulty with this topic and check up later that he really has understood it. As has been said previously, it is useful to calculate the difficulty level of each item in our tests. This shows us which points the children find difficult to grasp, or which points we have to think harder about how we should teach them next year.

If we use the project method in our teaching, e.g. study of work of the post office, collecting statistics, etc., we could use the next page to show which children have completed particular topics.

It is always useful to keep a record of your comments to parents. So the next page should be kept for these. Most schools report to parents three times a year. You will not be able to remember what you wrote for each child at Christmas when you are writing the Summer term report. Most parents keep their children's reports. It can be most embarrassing if a parent arrives showing you that you wrote 'Tunde always works consistently well' for the Easter report and then you wrote 'Tunde has done no work all year' for the Summer report!

It is useful to keep an additional couple of pages for remarks. These might include remarks on a child's progress, or any personal comment which you might think it is useful to remember or comment on the condition of the child which might affect his studies. Comments might range from 'Obi doesn't seem to have any friends' to 'Tunde doesn't seem to be able to see very well – ask parents' to 'Usman always needs pushing to do any work . . .'

Every now and again it is good practice to spend half an hour or so studying the records you have kept. In this way you get to know the children in your class better and you notice patterns. If Audu has had a whole row of good marks and then slowly gets worse marks there may be a reason. It may be he has just got too confident and become sloppy or it may be trouble at home. Noticing the change in the trend makes you aware of the problem. A problem noticed is a problem half solved. You may notice a child consistently gets low marks. If this continues for some time he will be convinced that he cannot do mathematics, and will not even try.

We should make a note to look more carefully at his next piece of work. We should try to find something we can congratulate him on even if it is only his layout. We may decide that he requires more carefully graded problems, and so on. The best way to put anyone off a subject is to consistently tell him he is no good. We, as teachers, sometimes forget that $\frac{2}{10}$ means 'You don't know so much do you!' but children never forget.

Records should not be considered as something we are told to do by the inspectors. They are a necessary part of teaching.

Organization in the Classroom

A well organized teacher is a contented teacher. A well organized teacher has more time to teach and the children learn more. Many hours of valuable teaching time are wasted because teachers do not give thought to organization.

Some of the organizational considerations may be thought of as quite petty, until we think about them. For example, how do we store and give out pencils? Many teachers keep pencils in a box; they rattle around and the leads get broken inside the wood, which leads to frustration and waste of time when we try to sharpen them. When we collect the pencils we have to count them – more waste of time. How can we organize distribution of pencils, scissors, etc. so that time is not wasted? Pencils may be given out four times a day. If we save two minutes on each distribution and collection we have saved 8 minutes a day, 40 minutes a week and about 20 hours over the year.

A simple method of storing pencils, scissors and the like is to store them in holes in a block of wood as in figure 9.3. We can see at a glance if they require sharpening. If there are 36 children in the class, bore 20 holes in two blocks of wood so that you have 4 spare sharpened pencils in reserve in case of breakages during the lesson.

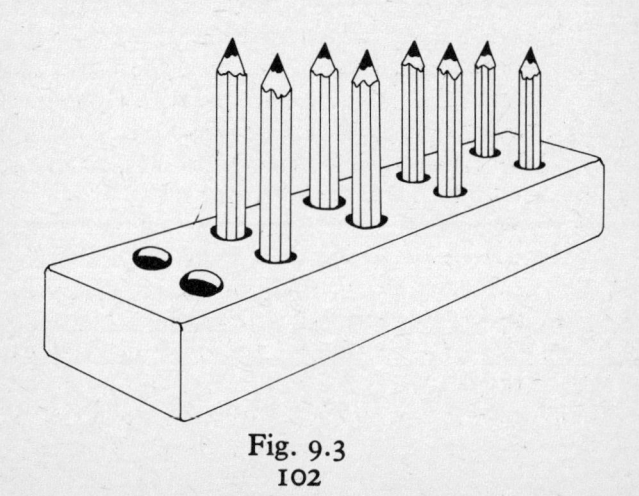

Fig. 9.3

The pencils can be given out by two children from the front row and perhaps collected by a different two children at the end of the lesson. The teacher can check at a glance that all pencils have been returned; an empty hole means a pencil not returned.

Giving out paper can take some time if we have not learnt how to 'fan' a stack of paper or fold the stack so that each sheet is separated from the next one and in 'steps' so that we can get hold of each sheet separately.

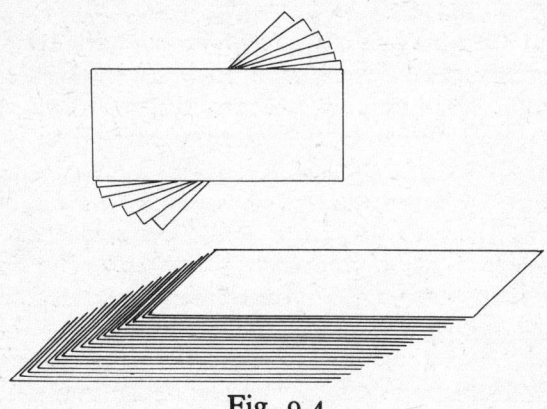

Fig. 9.4

The extent to which a teacher needs to be organized depends on the materials he is able to collect and buy and on the method of teaching he uses.

Let us consider the materials we would like to have in our classroom or available in the school to help us teach mathematics. We would like sheets of large paper to make wall charts, graph paper, squared paper, gummed coloured paper, plain paper, stiff card, felt pens, paints, drawing pins, coloured pencils, pencils, gum, plasticene, scissors, punch, sellotape, gummed tape, stapler, and so on. We would like boxes (chalk boxes will do), in which we can keep seeds and used matches in bundles. We would like a clock face to teach time, and aids to teach length, weight and volume (a collection of different containers, measuring jar, etc.), a thermometer and perhaps other materials for measuring rainfall, so that we can train the children in keeping records and perhaps drawing graphs. We would need pairs of compasses, protractors and so on in the top class. It would be useful to have a saw and a few simple tools, nails and screws so that we can make our own teaching aids. We have to keep spare exercise books. If masters are made for the duplicating machine we would like to store them for use next year. We might be able to obtain different sets of mathematics texts which we could use with the brighter or less gifted children, sets of mathematics cards, a mathematics dictionary might be useful . . . and so we could go on. If we have all this equipment it will have to be stored systematically so that we can find things.

If we are going to do experimental work, cutting out, making models etc., it would be useful to have at least a couple of flat topped desks. These would also be useful so that we could mount small exhibitions in one corner of the classroom.

If we are going to have the children working in groups we could reorganize the desks into groups of four so that the children have a larger surface area on which to work. There are many possibilities within a classroom if we think about it. Why should we take it for granted that the desks should be in rows and straight lines? We arrange our furniture in our homes to make a change, so why not in the classroom?

We should think about what responsibilities we can pass on to the children. If the children feel involved in the organization and running of the classroom they usually behave better and are in a more constructive and receptive mood. These responsibilities might be as small as shutting the door after the teacher enters, to helping the teacher with distributing or collecting exercise books, to helping the teacher make the necessary visual aids.

During practical lessons the class could be divided into groups of 4 as described on page 28. The idea under discussion on page 28 was that the groups gave the teacher the opportunity to do some social training. The grouping also helps in the organization of practical work. Only a quarter of the class is allowed to move when equipment is being distributed. The 'labourers' have the job of making sure the equipment is tidied away at the end of the lesson.

Exercises, Assignments and Projects
1 Visit a local primary school. Study the different types of records kept by teachers in different classes. Ask the headmaster if you can see what type of records he keeps for each child.

2 Make a collection of blank terminal report sheets used by different schools. Discuss their relative merits. Decide which you like the best and say why.
3 Imagine you have a free hand to buy what you like for a primary III class. Write a list of the equipment you would buy. You will have to study the syllabus to see what you require. Describe what storage facilities you would require.
4 Describe how you would organize an end of year test for a primary VI class.
5 Choose a topic from the primary syllabus which is suitable for a practical experiment which the children can do. Write a list of the equipment you would require. Explain how you would organize the distribution and collection of the material.
6 Have a discussion with a group of students in your year. Compete with each other, and try to convince the others that you will be the best organized teacher.

Chapter Ten

Difficulties Met by the Student Teacher and the New Teacher

Teaching Practice

Teaching practice is an important part of your training. It is an opportunity for you to try out the ideas you gleaned from your lecturers in College and your own reading.

You must appreciate, however, that you will not be in the position of a trained teacher. The teacher will have organized his scheme of work; his views may not be the same as yours. You must respect his views and advice even if you do not fully agree with them. As we have seen from our discussions the role of a teacher is a complex one; he is there to organize an environment in which the children can discover knowledge, and learn to use this knowledge to analyse and evaluate; to record the progress of children; to diagnose reasons for failure; to judge their ability and so on. No two teachers will ever come to the same opinion on how all these roles should be fulfilled. You should view your position as one of a helper and a learner rather than an organizer or initiator.

You are entering a society which has been established for many years. You have to conform to the standards of the school whether they be 'how you speak', 'what you wear' or 'if the children stand up when you come into the classroom'. You must find out the rules of the school, keep them yourself and insist that the children keep the rules relevant to them.

Discipline

Most student teachers are nervous when they first enter a classroom to see 40 pairs of eyes all looking at them. Will the children behave? So do not feel you are different if you feel nervous.

In the space provided in this book we can do little but offer advice. Whether a teacher has discipline problems or not depends on his attitude. If his lesson is well prepared, if he knows what he is going to do and what he expects the children to do, then he goes into the classroom concerned with communicating ideas. If there is any disturbance then he 'steps on it', not because of personal animosity between himself and a particular child but because the disturbance distracts the class from attaining their objectives. If the children see you want to get on with the job they will follow suit.

Some student teachers go into a class hoping to be friends with the children. You can be friendly but not friends. Friendship is something which grows; it can take months, years or sometimes it never happens. If you go into a class with this notion the children will regard you as soft and take advantage. You should go into the classroom with the notion that you are in charge and you are going to get some work done.

Organizing Yourself

Many of the problems of the student teacher are the same ones as those of the new teacher or even an experienced teacher going to a new school. You have to get to know a new environment, what and when you have to teach, what equipment you have to teach with, as much as you can about the children you are to teach and the general rules and organization of the school.

To help you with this task a check list is set out below. It is not exhaustive but should be of assistance.

The New Environment

Draw a plan of the school; don't forget the staff toilets. Are there special rooms for PE, art, science, or are all your classes in the same place? Whose job is it to keep the classroom clean, shut windows, lock the doors? Will the school be closed whilst you are on teaching practice (public holidays, etc.)? Will you miss any days teaching due to sports days and other similar functions?

What and When You Have To Teach

Find the times of periods making up the school time table; some schools have different times on different days. Find out which periods you will be expected to teach, what class you will be teaching and in what room. Is there a scheme of work for each period? Find out the work previously covered by the class or you will not know where to start. Are there any teachers' guides or teachers' syllabuses produced by the local Ministry of Education with special instructions or assistance?

Equipment

What type of exercise books do they use? Do they have a special note book? What text book do they use? Are copies of different text books available? Are there enough text books for each child? What space is available in the classroom for practical work? What display space is available? Are there pin boards or will you have to put a frame on wall charts so that you can hang them? What teaching aids are available in the classroom/college? Can the school secretary produce duplicating for you?

The Children

Obtain a list of the childrens' names. Make a mark book. Find out how the class teacher marks and what records he will expect you to keep. How many pieces of work are set per week? Produce class plans for each class you teach; write on them where each child sits. Find out as much as you can about the children in the class. Are there any pupils who will require special care or attention due to handicaps like illness or poor sight?

General Rules and Organization

What clothes are the children expected to wear? How are they expected to behave inside and outside the classroom?

Teaching Methods

Find out what methods of teaching are used. As stated in our previous discussions on methods of teaching, children do not respond to quick changes in methods. If the class teacher uses formal methods on most occasions don't be surprised if children are reluctant to answer questions if you are using the discussion or questioning method. If the children are used to sitting with their lips closed all day they will find it rather strange to be expected to answer questions all of a sudden.

The Area around the School

If you have an opportunity before teaching practice starts take a walk covering the area of a twenty minute walk from the school. You can usually find something of interest in the area which you can use in your teaching. Whether it be something you can use in your science lesson or a stimulus for a descriptive piece of writing or for mathematics.

The New Teacher

Many of the problems of the new teacher are the same as those previously mentioned for the student teacher. Some, however, are different. You will not be able to run away from the school after six weeks and leave your mistakes behind you. You have to work for the respect of the children in your class.

You are in control of your situation now; you can decide what methods of teaching you are going to use. It is up to you to think what materials you require for your teaching. You will have to find out what they cost and ask the head teacher to include them in his estimates for next year. You will have more time to get to know the children in your class. You will find that discipline is controlling separate children rather than controlling a 'class'.

You will realize in your second year of teaching that you didn't really prepare many lessons you gave in your first year properly, and you will realize that you are never fully satisfied with some lessons. We build and improve lessons year by year.

Exercises, Assignments and Projects

1. Discuss the difference between being friends and being friendly. Show how this should affect your attitude to children.
2. Make a case study of a local primary school. Discuss any good points about the school. Explain how the school could be improved within reasonable cost.
3. See if your tutor can invite groups of (a) teachers with one year's experience, (b) teachers with several years of experience to the College. Arrange to hold discussions on methods of teaching, building lessons over the years, discipline problems, topics which are found difficult to teach, and so on.
    You can learn a great deal in any walk of life by talking to people with experience.

Chapter Eleven

Evaluating Our Teaching

To a certain extent we are evaluating our skill as a teacher when we give the children a test. We are testing how successful we have been in communicating our ideas. If the children cannot obtain the correct solution the logical conclusion is that they have not learnt the concepts we have taught. The excuse of many teachers at this point is 'Oh well, of course those children are not very bright'. Our test, perhaps, has shown us that we are not very successful at communicating with the dull child; or we are covering the material too quickly for them to understand; or we do not understand the difficulties a child has with a particular topic because we have not broken it down into separate difficulties in our teaching.

If 75% of the class obtained more than 60% in a test or in worked examples given straight after a lesson we could say we have done very well. But what of the 25% who obtained marks below 60%? Are these always the same children? If they are should we consider taking them as a separate group? With more detailed explanations and more finely graded problems they should learn some useful mathematics.

If 75% of the class obtain less than 50% in a test given on subject matter just taught, then there is no doubt that we have failed to communicate our ideas. It is not much of an excuse to say 'Yes, but some children obtained high marks'. Those children would no doubt have obtained the same mark if you had told them to read their text book on their own.

Testing the children will, therefore, give us a rough idea as to whether we are good, bad or indifferent but it will not tell us what we can do to improve. We have to develop the ability to watch the children and recognize the effect of our teaching on them. We have to develop the ability to criticize ourselves. As said in Chapter One, for most of the time a teacher is his own boss. There is no-one to tell the teacher what he is doing wrong. There is no-one to tell him how to improve his teaching. If a teacher wishes to improve his teaching he must develop the habit of criticizing each lesson after he has given it.

This is easier said than done. Often whilst supervising teaching practice or inspecting schools I have asked teachers to criticize the lesson which they have just given. In most cases the answer has been 'Oh it went well'. What they really meant is that the children behaved and the teacher got through the material he intended to do. The difficulty in criticizing yourself is that if you have done what you planned then you think everything has gone well. The real question we have to ask is 'Could we have done better? Did as many children as possible learn as much as possible? If not, what could we have "done" better? How could we have improved our communication?'

Remember communication depends on how the teacher organizes the learning situation and on the willingness of the learner to receive the communication.

Can we develop a method by means of which we can learn to criticize ourselves? The main difficulty is that there are so many aspects which can affect the learning situation. We have not got the time to go through a long list of questions at the end of each lesson.

List of Questions To Ask

There follows: *A* – a long list of questions which you might go through every now and again, and *B* – a shorter list which you could ask yourself as you are leaving the classroom.

A

1. Did I fully understand what I was teaching? Could I explain the concepts I was trying to teach in clear, concise language?
2. Did the subject matter follow logically from previous knowledge which the children had? Did some children have difficulty with the knowledge I assumed they knew? Did I link the subject with other school subjects?
3. Was the introduction to the lesson well prepared and presented? Did I obtain the children's interest in what they were going to study?
4. What kind of a mood was I in? Did I produce a healthy learning atmosphere? Were the children over-anxious or 'scared stiff'?
5. Were my objectives well thought out? Was I sure what I

was aiming at and how I was going to obtain my objectives throughout the lesson? Did I find myself having to think ahead as I knew I was heading for a difficulty I had not previously thought about?

6 Were the children given a clear picture of what we were going to study during the lesson? Were they given a framework to which they could add as the lesson progressed?

7 Did the lesson flow? Did I cover the content in logical order? Did the lesson have a story?

8 Did I find that any particular points were difficult to get over? Was there a need for more teaching aids? Did the children understand what we were doing? Were there any words used which the children found difficult to understand? Am I sure that the children understood the meanings of the new words and will remember their meanings? Could all the children read and pronounce the new words by the end of the lesson?

9 Were the children involved in the lesson? Did I talk too much? Did I expect the children to sit there like sponges absorbing my clever words without any thought? Did I ask the children any questions? Were my questions purely factual questions or did they make the children think? Did I listen to the answers given by the children with interest? Did I make use of their answers to further the lesson? If an answer given was wrong, did I just disregard it with disgust or did I ask the child another question which would help the child to give the right answer?

10 Were the children interested and attentive throughout the lesson? Did they all work hard? Why did some children not attend? Is it always the same children who do not attend? Were the less bright children fully occupied during the lesson?

11 Were any children particularly difficult during the lesson? Was I unjust in my treatment of any particular child? Do I think the children respect me more or less after the lesson? Do they think I am a good controller and mediator of the social situation in the classroom? Was there any particular child who has to be congratulated or 'stamped on' next lesson? Were any disturbances my own fault? Did I upset anyone's feelings?

12 Could the lesson have been better organized? Was time wasted? Could things be better organized next time?
13 What did the chalkboard look like at the end of the lesson? Should some of the things written on the chalk board have been written on a wall chart so that they could be left on the wall for the children to make future reference?
14 Did I summarize the lesson at the end? Did the children write some kind of notes on the main points of the lesson to which they can refer in the future? Did I give any homework? If not, would it have been useful to give some?
15 Did the children enjoy the lesson? Did I enjoy the lesson? Were the children convinced that the lesson was useful and/or worthwhile?
16 Did I evaluate how successfully the children had learnt the lesson? Where do I start next time? Are there any children who need a little personal help?
17 Was there too much or too little material in the lesson? Did I talk too quickly at any time during the lesson? Do I talk with enthusiasm or in a bored tone? Did I keep to the point?
18 Did I choose the right method for teaching the lesson? Could the lesson have been more child-centred? Did I learn anything during the lesson? Could improvements be made to the lesson when it is taught next year?
19 How long is it since I have done any revision of material taught? Would it be useful to have a revision period? Is it time I gave a periodic test so that the children will revise their work?

There are many more questions which one could ask. The questions above are sufficient to show what a complex business teaching is.

If one asked all these questions at the end of every lesson we would be half an hour late for the next lesson. If, however, a teacher does wish to improve his teaching he should periodically question himself on his ability.

The shorter list below shows questions which should be asked at the conclusion of every lesson.

B
1 Did I know what I was talking about?

2 What success did I have in communicating the new ideas to the children?
3 Could I have used a better method of teaching?
4 What were the main difficulties encountered in communicating the ideas?
5 Where do I start the next lesson? (Make a note of this.)
6 Have I improved my relationship with the children during this lesson?

Exercises, Assignments and Projects
1 When you are on teaching practice watch a lesson given by one of your fellow students. Write a report on his teaching using the questions asked about the ability of a teacher in this chapter. Allow your fellow student to watch a lesson given by you. Ask him to report on your teaching.
2 Do you think the short list of questions covers the most important aspects of the lesson? Explain why you think the questions are important. Add any further questions which you think should be asked at the conclusion of a lesson.

Chapter Twelve

Revision Questions

1. Explain what you mean by
   - (a) place value,
   - (b) a decimal,
   - (c) a fraction,
   - (d) area,
   - (e) volume,
   - (f) an angle,
   - (g) a rectangular solid,
   - (h) a plane figure.
2. Discuss how you would convince someone that mathematics is an essential part of the school curriculum.
3. Study the primary syllabus and decide what topics you think could be left out if all primary school children continued to Secondary Education.
4. As many children finish their formal education at the end of primary school it is essential that they have an understanding of the mathematics they will need in their lives by the time they leave. Make a study of the mathemattics you think they will need in their lives. Compare your list with the primary school mathematics syllabus.
5. Devise a method for preparing a lesson. Your starting point could be analysing how the topic is presented in a text book. Explain how you would like to prepare lessons.
6. Consider you have been asked to give a talk on 'Teaching Aids in Mathematics Teaching' to a group of practising teachers. Describe what you would say.
7. Describe, and illustrate, three different ways of teaching a primary mathematics topic of your choice. Decide which method you think is the best and explain why.
8. State the different types of records you think a mathematics teacher should keep on his students. Explain why you think a teacher should keep the records you have mentioned, and the use to which these records should be put.
9. In most classes in which we teach there is a wide range of

abilities. Discuss how you would organize your subject matter and your teaching to take account of this.

10 'A test should be reliable and valid.' 'A test should be designed for a specific purpose.' Explain what you think is meant by these statements. Describe how you would construct a test for a particular purpose, and state what precautions you would take to ensure that the test is reliable and valid.

11 'The mathematics we teach in school should be relevant to the life our children are living at present.' Discuss to what extent you think this statement can be accepted. Show to what extent a teacher can make his mathematics teaching relevant to the children's present life.

12 A mark for a test has no meaning when stated on its own. Discuss why this is so and describe a process which could be used to ensure the reported mark has meaning.

13 'A teacher is a professional organizer.' Discuss this statement.

14 Many schools run a banking system for pocket money. Describe as briefly as possible how you would organize this system. Describe what the children will learn by using the system. Discuss whether you think the idea is worthwhile.

Sources of Information and Materials

Information
1. The Nigerian Educational Research Council (NERC), P.O. Box 8058, Yaba, Lagos.
2. The Mathematics Teachers' Association of Nigeria (MTAN).
3. The Mathematics Association of Nigeria (MAN).
4. The West African Examination Council (WAEC): The Senior Deputy Registrar, WAEC, PMB 1022, Yaba, Lagos.
5. The Mathematics Inspector of your local Ministry of Education.

Books, Work Cards and Other Materials
1. African University Press, 305 Herbert Macauley Street, PMB 3560, Yaba, Lagos.
2. Allen and Unwin, Nigeria Publishers Services Ltd., P.O. Box 62, Ibadan.
3. Cambridge University Press, Nigeria Publishers Services Ltd., P.O. Box 62, Ibadan.
4. Evans Brothers (Nigeria Publishers) Ltd., PMB 5164, Jericho Road, Ibadan.
5. Heinemann Educational Books Ltd., PMB 5205, Ighodaro Road, Jericho, Ibadan.
6. Longmans Nigeria Ltd., 52 Oba Akran Avenue, PMB 21036, Ikeja, Lagos.
7. Macmillan Nigeria Publishers Ltd., P.O. Box 264, Industrial Avenue, Ilupeju Estate, Yaba, Lagos.
8. Thomas Nelson (Nigeria) Ltd., Nelson House, 8 Ilupeju Bypass, PMB 21303, Ikeja, Lagos.
9. Hodder and Stoughton Educational, Nigeria Publishers Services, P.O. Box 62, Ibadan.
10. Onibonoje, P.O. Box 3109, Ibadan.
11. University Press Ltd., PMB 5095, Oxford House, Iddo Gate, Ibadan.

Teaching Aids
U.K.
1. E. J. Arnolds and Sons Ltd.:
   Export Sales Manager, Butterley Street, Leeds LS10 1AX, England.
2. Invicta Plastics Ltd.:
   Educational Aids Division, Oadby, Leicester LE2 4LB, England.
3. Osmiroid Educational:
   Osmiroid Works, Gosport, Hampshire, England.
4. Six to Twelve:
   Incorporating Metric Aids Ltd., Medway House, Faircharm Industrial Estate, Evelyn Drive, Leicester LE3 2BU, England.
5. Taskmaster Ltd.:
   Morris Road, Leicester LE2 6BR, England.

Tests (Standardized)
1. National Foundation for Educational Research in England and Wales:
   The Mere, Upton Park, Slough, Bucks, England.
2. Harcourt, Brace, Jovanovich Inc., Test Dept.,
   757 Third Avenue, New York, New York 10017.
3. George G. Harrap & Co. Ltd. (Attainment Tests):
   182 High Holborn, London.